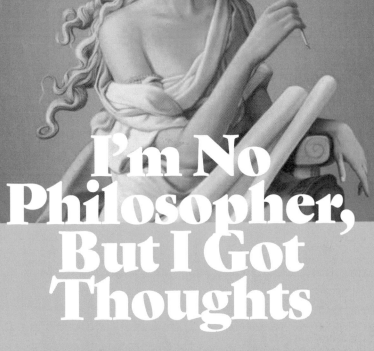

KRISTIN CHENOWETH

I'm No Philosopher, But I Got Thoughts

MINI MEDITATIONS FOR SAINTS, SINNERS, AND THE REST OF US

HARPER
Celebrate

To my family and friends, who hold me tight.
To Josh, who holds me upright.
To the Glitter Girls, who hold me in their hearts.

A SIMPLE PRAYER
FOR THIS BOOK

Creator,
open my mind to create.

Christ,
open my heart to love.

Holy Spirit,
empower my voice.

CONTENTS

Foreword viii
Introduction xiii

chapter one THOUGHTS ABOUT QUESTIONING 1

chapter two THOUGHTS ABOUT BELONGING 11

chapter three THOUGHTS ABOUT HUMBLE PIE 23

chapter four THOUGHTS ABOUT VERTIGO 35

chapter five THOUGHTS ABOUT OPENNESS 51

chapter six THOUGHTS ABOUT CONNECTION 65

chapter seven THOUGHTS ABOUT LOVING 75

chapter eight THOUGHTS ABOUT WORK 87

chapter nine THOUGHTS ABOUT DISRUPTION 101

chapter ten THOUGHTS ABOUT WHAT FITS 117

chapter eleven THOUGHTS ABOUT SCREWING UP 127

chapter twelve THOUGHTS ABOUT HARMONY 139

chapter thirteen THOUGHTS ABOUT LOSS 153

chapter fourteen THOUGHTS ABOUT OPPORTUNITY 165

chapter fifteen THOUGHTS ABOUT ANXIETY 179

chapter sixteen THOUGHTS ABOUT CLOSURE 189

Afterword 200
Acknowledgments 202
About the Author 204

FOREWORD

I've never written a foreword before, but if there's anything I just might be equipped for, it's talking about how much I love Kristin Chenoweth. The first time I saw Kristin perform live was at a concert in my hometown, Boca Raton, Florida, singing with the Florida Sunshine Pops. I remember seeing for the first time all the things that I loved embodied in one tiny human: stunning high notes, effortless funny, and so much heart—heart bigger than her physical entirety, but perhaps not her heels. Shortly after this, I was cast at the Little Palm Family Theatre in a production of *You're a Good Man, Charlie Brown* as Sally Brown—Kristin's Tony Award–winning role. Between seeing her in concert and studying her beloved and iconic performance as Sally, she very quickly became one of my idols.

The first time I met Kristin, I was ten years old. My mom took me to see *Wicked* at the Gershwin Theatre, and I won a backstage pass during a Broadway Cares/Equity Fights AIDS live auction after the show. My mom couldn't have stopped me from bidding on this backstage pass if she had duct-taped my hands to the bottom of the seat. I anxiously waited in the hallway lined with dressing room doors. And then Kristin's opened up! Fresh-faced in a T-shirt and jeans, kinder and bubblier and warmer than one could hope or imagine. She welcomed my family and me into her dressing room. Her dog peed on the couch, and I helped her clean it up (a life high-light). She asked me questions and listened carefully when I responded (as if ten-year-old me had anything truly magnificent to say); she filled my arms with gifts (a small wand and a glittery shower gel that I savored, using tiny drops every day for a few years to follow); and then she sent me on my way.

As I floated home, something became very clear to me. Kristin Chenoweth is unimaginably just as impressive, if not even more so, as a human being than she is as an artist. This became truer and clearer to me as time went on and our paths crossed again. I had the incredible honor of working alongside her in *Hairspray Live!* on NBC in 2016, watching her pitch endless new bits, reinterpret jokes, and ask a question that changed my life: "Does this add value?" She applied this test to every inch of the material.

I had assumed we already knew Miss Baltimore Crabs, and we did. Just not Kristin's Miss Baltimore Crabs. She made choices that were courageous and smart, as always. She came up with endless new bits that she knew were brilliantly funny but delivered them honestly and landed them with ease, as always. Watching her entirely rewrite this role in real time was a master class, and I had never been so grateful to be the student.

It's not often that we get to befriend our idols, but that's what happened for me. We worked together. We checked on each other often. We grew to be true friends. She makes me feel cared for, the same way I felt in her dressing room when I was ten years old. She has held my hand through some of the very hardest times of my life and has taught me by example how to survive as a heartful woman in an often heartless industry and how to transform the heaviness into light.

There is much more to say and to share, but I know you are probably just as excited to begin reading this book as I am, so I suppose I just wanted to confirm for you that however brilliant and kind you think she is, *she really is*. A million times more over. Unconditionally. As an artist, as a human.

I hope this book allows you to feel even more of the magic that is Kristin the human. She truly is the goodliest witch there is.

Ariana Grande
Los Angeles, California
2022

INTRODUCTION

Who are we trying to kid? When it comes to spirituality, we're all a bunch of baby goats looking for a hug and a hot yoga class. My mission in this little book is not to revolutionize your worldview; my mission is to provoke a giggle, encourage a blink, and remind you that God's hand has a light touch. I'll share a few stories about my work and family and provide space for you to process stories, thoughts, and questions of your own. As with line dancing and life in general, it's more fun when we do it together.

I'm no philosopher, but I've played one on TV. And in the movies. And on Broadway. Every character I've ever played has her own unique worldview, and cracking that open was key to playing the bejeebers out of her.

Cunégonde has an athletic tour de force number in *Candide* that embodies the hard work of happiness. Olive Snook in *Pushing Daisies* went full zen when she sang about building "a little birdhouse in your soul." Sally Brown's "My New Philosophy" in *You're a Good Man, Charlie Brown* is a sweet little dune buggy of a number that won me my first Tony. In it, Sally explains her very specific credo to Schroeder: "Some philosophies pick and choose, deciding what goes in it. Some take a lifetime; mine take a minute!" It's hilarious, but come on, if a minute is all you got, you can't go wrong with a deep breath and a moment of clarity.

These are seeds that grow, and my worldview is a flower bed. A marigold here. A daffodil there. I'm not trying to tell anybody what to believe. I just happen to believe that—for myself—there's some good in a moment of reflection now and then. Like Olive, Cunégonde, and Sally, I've cultivated my unique worldview. Thank you for inviting me into your day and letting me share a few of my thinky thoughts with you.

Thoughts about career.

Thoughts about love.

Thoughts about purpose.

Thoughts about how we inhabit these bodies, these families, and this world God has invited us to dwell in.

I know you don't have time or bandwidth to get lost in the meanderings of Maimonides or the navel-gazing of Nietzsche. If you do, congrats! Maybe I'll see you on that mountaintop someday. Meanwhile, I find a pithy meme of forty characters or less is more my speed. You know—the kind of deep thought that belongs in a Hallmark card but for the sake of gravitas is always attributed to T. S. Eliot or Lao Tzu.

"Be kind. I don't wanna have to pray for you." —Susan B. Anthony

"This shiz writes itself." —Mark Twain

"The unexamined life is not worth living." —Paris Hilton

Okay, that last one actually came from Socrates, but Paris Hilton puts a whole new spin on it, right? And yes, we're allowed to do that. The legacy of great thinkers should be more than great thoughts; it should also be the inspiration to think great thoughts of our own. Good ideas should evolve as we apply them to our evolving world.

In short—all puns intended—this book is my gift to you: a celebration of whatever makes this day joyful, a mini-vacation from whatever makes it a challenge. Please know that all my high hopes and gratitude come with it.

Love, Kristin

WHO SAID IT BEST?

William James

"There is only one thing that a philosopher can be relied on to do . . . a philosopher can contradict other philosophers."

Sally Brown

"Oh yeah? That's what *you* think!"

Somewhere beyond right and wrong,
there is a garden.
I will meet you there.

When the soul lies down
in that grass,
the world is too full to talk about.
Even the words each other
make no sense.

Doodle Time

SUBDIVISION OF MY MENTAL REAL ESTATE

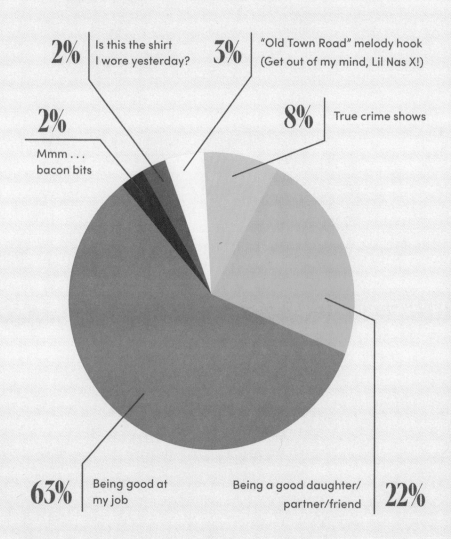

2% Is this the shirt I wore yesterday?

3% "Old Town Road" melody hook (Get out of my mind, Lil Nas X!)

2% Mmm . . . bacon bits

8% True crime shows

63% Being good at my job

22% Being a good daughter/ partner/friend

BUT FOR REAL...

What's occupying your thoughts? Slice up the pie chart, and ask yourself: "How do I feel about the expenditure of my time and emotional energy? Am I getting a good return on my investment?" Remind yourself as you divvy up this pie chart: "I draw the lines."

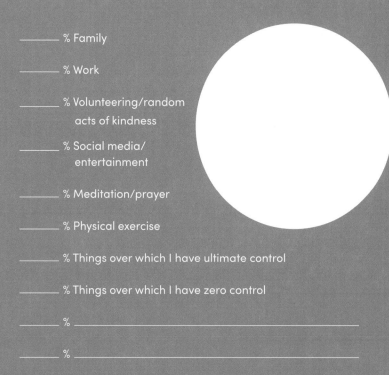

_____ % Family

_____ % Work

_____ % Volunteering/random acts of kindness

_____ % Social media/ entertainment

_____ % Meditation/prayer

_____ % Physical exercise

_____ % Things over which I have ultimate control

_____ % Things over which I have zero control

_____ % _____

_____ % _____

THOUGH
QUE

TS ABOUT
STIONING

One of the first solos I sang in church was Bill and Gloria Gaither's "Jesus, I Heard You Had a Big House." The song is a wide-open door, welcoming everyone into the light of the Lord's love. I was small enough to fit into a soup can, but I belted that sucker out, and there was not a dry eye in the place.

Somebody was visiting from Tulsa, and they invited me to come and sing at their church, and somebody at their church heard me, and before long, I got to be kind of a hot ticket. Churches all over Oklahoma were asking me to sing, so almost every Sunday, my family would go to Enid or Beggs or Locust Grove.

My dad bought a little sound system we packed around with us, because sometimes the church's system was a bit janky, and he knew how much I cared about delivering the goods to the best of my ability. I didn't think of myself as any sort of missionary; I was just being me—"that little girl with the big voice" people kept talking about.

Because we visited a range of churches on the Christian spectrum, I was exposed to a lot of different styles of worship and a range of beliefs that set the stage for a lot of questions. I was intrigued, even then, by the way some preachers thundered old-time brimstone and damnation while others wooed their flocks with parables about mustard seeds and hidden talents. Some sermons seemed preoccupied with assigning certain people to hell, while others were more interested in lifting everyone up with colorful felt banners, the Love Chapter, and lemon bars in the fellowship hall.

In 1980 I was invited to sing at the Southern Baptist Convention in Tulsa. An audience of ten thousand people. At the time, I was focused on singing—preferably without tossing my cookies. I was so nervous. All those people! But I got through it, and the experience was life-changing for me as a young performer. I didn't know or care anything about the resolutions being debated at that convention: broad resolutions and sweeping condemnations of scientific

FRIENDLY REMINDER

You know how people tell you to

have the "patience of Job"?

Well, I checked my Bible, and Job

bitched his head off.

So there ya go. You now have

the patience of Job.

You're welcome.

thought, homosexuality, human rights for children, and the equality of women.

As a teen, I started reading and thinking beyond that sort of spoon-fed dogma, and it unsettled me. How could I be a good Christian if some parts of the Bible—or certain interpretations of the Bible—just didn't sit right in my stomach? My Grandma Chenoweth, a big Bible reader, was untroubled by the contradictory mandates and inconsistent stories within it.

"I eat the fish without choking on the bones," she said.

These days, whenever people accuse me of cherry-picking which parts of the Bible I apply to my life, I think of that wise little tidbit I inherited from my grandmother. She taught me to listen to the ideas of others but trust my own heart and design my own belief system. The Bible, she reminded me, is not a single book; it's a library. Not everyone hangs out in the same section of the stacks.

Eat the fish. Leave the bones.

Receive nourishment from whatever nourishes you. Sidestep the choking hazards. Those bones were necessary for the fish, but you'll never be able to comfortably swallow them.

This healthy directive can be applied to just about anything, including (but not limited to) Scripture, fashion magazines, friendly advice (solicited or unsolicited), and the entire cannon of bons mots and bumper stickers we all get bombarded with every day on social media. Think of all that input—including this little book—as a platter of crunchy-coated fish sticks. Snack on it as needed. Just for the halibut. (*Ba-dum-bum-CHH*!) If an idea resonates for you, chew on it. If not, that's fine. There's no need to argue about it. Discreetly spit it into your napkin and move along, Gladys. Me and Mrs. Paul—we just want you to be happy.

Nobody has all the answers. Even Jesus didn't give us a straight-up rule book. He gave us stories and encouraged us to ask questions.

"Search the Scriptures," He said in the Gospel of John.

He told us to explore for ourselves, because the figuring out part is how we grow. Forget about knowing all the answers; the object of the game is to know *yourself*.

If you insist on knowing all the answers in life, you're going to be (a) disappointed and (b) no fun to sit next to on an airplane. It's about the process. The journey, if you will.

And I will! Why not?

I actually find questions a lot more interesting than answers. Questions are usually honest while answers are frequently BS. A question is a starting point, a door that swings open and invites a host of ideas to stop by for a Coke and fried Oreos.

So turn the page and let's get interrogative.

*I want
to know.*

*I'm willing
to know.*

*I'm waiting
to know.*

Y'know?

Sell your
CLEVERNESS
and buy
BEWILDERMENT.

Rumi

QUESTIONS FOR GOD
WHEN I MEET HIM: PART 2

In *A Little Bit Wicked*, I shared a list of QFGWIMH:

- Why is forgiveness so dang hard?
- Why is slapstick so dang funny?
- *Who* is the sadistic genius behind cellulite?
- Where are the mates to most of my socks?
- What if you made it so that hate would cause hemorrhoids? Just an idea.

Believe me, that list has grown as long as an opera glove during the decade since that book was published.

- Will there be a welcome event? (If so, please make sure I'm seated between Flo Bird and Maria Tallchief.)
- Where are all the angels? I'm talking database with GPS. People need to know.
- If happy little bluebirds fly beyond the rainbow— okay, never mind.
- Is it me?

WHILE I CONTINUE MY LIST, I INVITE YOU TO START A LIST OF
YOUR OWN. HERE'S A LITTLE JUMP START.

Dear God:

Where were you when . . .

Why do you always seem so . . .

What would happen if I . . .

How much longer do I have to wait for . . .

And another thing:

TS ABOUT LONGING

I always knew I was adopted, but I also knew I was exactly where I belonged. My wonderful mom and dad, Junie and Jerry Chenoweth, took me home a few days after I was born, and from that moment, I was their baby girl, richly blessed, dearly loved, never wanting for anything. My family was my family—Mom, Dad, my brother Mark, and me—every one of us perfectly imperfect in a way that fit together like a sweetly crazy, little can of fruit cocktail.

Much like your family, I'm guessing.

We've been through some stuff, but whatever's happening downstage center—laughing, crying, chemo, or a spirited game of Candy Land—there's always love in the background.

"IF WE HAVE NO PEACE, IT IS BECAUSE WE HAVE FORGOTTEN THAT WE BELONG TO EACH OTHER."

MOTHER TERESA

My parents recognized a unique gift in me and made it possible for me to take my talent as far as anyone could have taken it. They gave me a firm foundation of faith, a solid rock I could cling to when things got rough. They showed up for me. They believed in me. They had my back. They supported my decision to pursue the most impractical path and helped me find my way to a life-changing mentor, who helped me find my way into professional life.

I've worked really hard, but that's okay. I'm a hard worker. That's who I am. And in the Broadway community, I found an incredibly hardworking tribe. I *belonged* on Broadway, and Broadway *belonged* me back. I've had to reinvent myself more times than I can count, but I keep finding my way back to my tribe, one way or another.

Belonging is not the same thing as acceptance. It doesn't depend on someone else's approval—like being allowed to sit at the lunch table with the mean girls. It's a feeling you recognize within yourself, and it's contagious. Other people pick up on that sense of belonging, and the universe seems to shift accordingly.

> Belonging is not the same thing as acceptance.

It doesn't always work that way, of course, especially in this Business we call *Show*. So many people strive so hard, and some never get the breaks.

Others seem to have arrived—they appear to have the whole world in their pockets—but they can't enjoy it because on some sad gut level, they never really believe they deserve it.

The sting of rejection is the evil twin of that sense of belonging, and in those moments, the pain is proof of one thing: you got the belonging right. You knew what you needed, and you went for it.

That's a super crappy consolation prize, of course. Let's just acknowledge that it sucks to have your heart broken, personally or professionally. Heartbreak is a *B-I-sharkbite-bitch*. I know this from a wealth of heartbreaking experience—moments when there was no consolation prize, only another mountain to climb. But I have seen from a variety of mountaintops that anyone who cruises through life without getting their heart broken probably isn't loving hard enough.

> Anyone who cruises through life without getting their heart broken probably isn't loving hard enough.

It's tempting to shy away from that level of belonging that makes you vulnerable to factors you can't control. But the wealth of heartbreak in my life resulted from a wealth of love, and the love was so good, the fear of heartbreak doesn't hold me back.

That's right. I'm talkin' to you, Heartbreak. I'll call your bad romance and raise you a *Madame Butterfly*. I ain't scared.

The takeaway from any heartbreak, I suppose, is that you know yourself well enough to know where and when to start over, and that puts you a lot closer to being right where you belong.

"True belonging only happens when we present our authentic, imperfect selves to the world," Brené Brown says in *Braving the Wilderness*. "Our sense of belonging can never be greater than our level of self-acceptance."

A SIMPLE PRAYER
FOR MY FAMILY

I know you see us.

Help us see each other.

*When ill-chosen words
get in the way,*

*help us bear the loving
intent behind them.*

*When old injuries
get in the way,*

help us promote healing.

*When we can't get out
of our own heads,*

*help us keep each
other in our hearts.*

ZEN VENN *Fix / Worry*

THINGS I
CAN FIX

THINGS I
WORRY ABOUT

THINGS I
CAN'T FIX

UNDERBITE

MESSY DESK

UNRULY DOG
BEHAVIOR

DRY SKIN

BAD HAIR

WORLD PEACE

MY INSOMNIA

MY CAR

LARGE
APPLIANCES

GLOBAL
PANDEMIC

OTHER PEOPLE'S
PROBLEMS

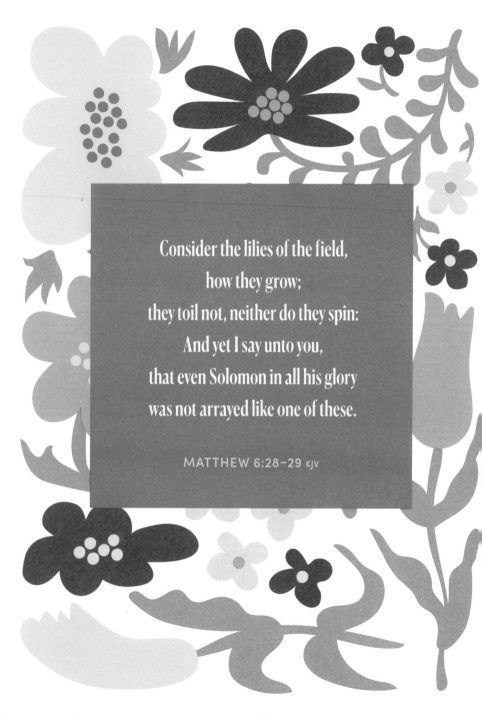

Consider the lilies of the field,
how they grow;
they toil not, neither do they spin:
And yet I say unto you,
that even Solomon in all his glory
was not arrayed like one of these.

MATTHEW 6:28–29 KJV

Flip the Script

I'M TRYING TO REWRITE THE NEGATIVE
DIALOGUE THAT COMES OUT OF HABIT.

INSTEAD OF SAYING . . .	I TRY TO SAY . . .
"Sorry for the slow reply."	"Thank you for your patience."
"I'm so stupid."	"I love your idea."
"I'm too [short/skinny/wrong] for this outfit."	"This doesn't fit me."
"You're such an idiot."	"I don't understand you."
"You don't care how I feel."	"You're not hearing me."
"I hate myself for procrastinating."	"To everything there is a season. And right now, it's *take care of me* time."

WHEN IN DOUBT:

Think

WW DOUBLE D!

(What would Dolly do?)

From the cowardice that dare not face new truth,

from the laziness that is contented with half truth,

from the arrogance that thinks it knows all truth,

Good God, deliver me!

THOUGH
HU

TS ABOUT
MBLE PIE

My very first day in Florence Birdwell's class, she said, "I'm going to have one of our upperclassmen sing for you in a moment. I want everyone to know where they're headed. But before we do that, I'm going to ask Kristi Chenoweth to sing."

Uh . . . hummana-hummana-wha?

She was putting me up there with someone I knew to be her star pupil. On my first day. Because apparently, I was just that good.

Feeling pretty chuffed about the whole thing, I went to the accompanist and gave him a few brief instructions, and then I went to the front of the room and delivered my exuberant eighteen-year-old first-day-of-school rendition of "New York, New York."

A lot of people were belting that song at a lot of auditions at the time, because that song is just . . . a lot. I knew I could belt it out bigger, louder, and a-lotter than any of those other little Pippin-heads, and I owned it.

Owned. It.

Wow-point-*oh!* on the Richter scale.

Those little-town blues—they were melting away. I think I saw a crack appear in the ceiling. Plaster dust sprinkling down.

Go, little eighteen-year-old me!

I hauled that sucker in with a big finish, and everybody applauded like crazy. Everyone except Flo Bird. She pressed her hand to her heart and said, "Oh. I can't wait to teach you how to sing."

And then the star pupil got up there and delivered some transcendent Puccini wrecking ball of an aria, and I was like, *Ah. I see what you did there.* This was a "before" and "after" type thing, and there was zero doubt about which one of us was the unbleached muslin in the tie-dye demonstration. I was left standing there like a raw potato on *Top Chef*—full of starch and fresh potential.

I knew I could sing. No one could take that from me— and that was never Flo Bird's intention. Her intention was to prove to me that there was a better way to use my instrument, and in order to do that, she had to feed me a slice of humble pie, which the star soprano served up with a side of Cool Whip.

Swallowing that was painful. I was humbled, and being humbled is unpleasant in the moment, but if we're willing to unwrap it like the gift it is, it can be transformative.

Now, just to clarify—*Danger, Will Robinson! Danger!*— I'm not talking about *humiliation*. Humiliating another person is never okay, and it's particularly egregious when you're talking about a kid.

There's a difference between *humiliation* and *humility*.

Humiliation lies. Humility speaks truth.

Humiliation silences you. Humility empowers you.

Humiliation is a byproduct of conflict with someone else. Humility is a byproduct of peace within yourself.

> I was humbled, and being humbled is unpleasant in the moment, but if we're willing to unwrap it like the gift it is, it can be transformative.

The goal of humiliation is to make you hate yourself. Humility requires us to love our *me of the moment* selves with compassion and good humor, making way for better selves we know we can be.

Humiliation is a weapon, slung in anger, incited by fear. Humility is a schoolbook, offered in hope, motivated by love—hopefully, with a side of Cool Whip.

There's a great moment in Luke 14 when Jesus was out to dinner with his disciples, and they were all jockeying and nudging, trying to sit next to Him and the wealthy person who was hosting the banquet. Jesus told them, "Simmer down, y'all. If you bulldoze your way to the head of the table, chances are the host will come along and tell you to move aside for someone more important. Take a seat at the foot of the table and hang out until someone invites you to move up. Meanwhile, it's more fun hanging out with regular folks anyway, so get over yourselves, and let's eat."

Yes, I'm paraphrasing, but I'm pretty sure that was true to tone.

It's hard to reconcile that advice with the constant hand-waving of social media. Being seen is now a hobby, a business, a monetized obsession. Ever since *platform* became a verb, the desire to be noticed has overtaken the desire to be noteworthy. Everybody's clamoring for attention, craving that seat at the head of the table. Perform first; pay attention later.

"Visibility these days seems to somehow equate to success," Michaela Coel said when she accepted her 2021 Emmy for writing *I May Destroy You*. "Do not be afraid to disappear

get over yourselves, and let's eat

from it, from us, for a while, and see what comes to you in the silence."

She nailed it, didn't she?

. . . afraid to disappear . . .

The reflex that compelled the disciples to jostle for a spotlight seat at the table is the same thing that compels us to Instagram our damn Corn Flakes—*fear of disappearing*—and in that environment, humility is an act of supreme courage.

The need for attention is a hungry little skeeter that doesn't care where it gets its next gulp of iron-rich blood. It could be from the deliciously exposed cleavage of Gisele Bündchen or it could be from a dog's butt. Whether you're loving or being loved, there's a difference between a click and actual caring. I worry that we're settling for a very dog-butt level of affection a lot of the time, simply because we feel the itch of this need to be seen—to be a part of something—and we've been offered this stupidly easy way to scratch it.

> The need for attention is a hungry little skeeter that doesn't care where it gets its next gulp of iron-rich blood.

I also worry that young performers internalize criticism and/or outright hate that comes their way without evaluating context. "Consider the source" is the first rule of evaluating and applying constructive criticism on stage, on the page, in the fitting room mirror, and in the perilous territory of the smartphone.

Ironically, humility is possible only when we love ourselves—as we are, as we have been, as we hope to be—independent of the approval or disapproval of anyone else.

So lately I've been asking myself:

- Am I allowing the knee-jerk likes/dislikes of other people to inform my ability to like myself?
- Am I settling for love that doesn't live up to the word?
- Do I have the guts to take a seat and let my work speak for me?
- Can I accept and celebrate myself as *enough* in the presence of only me, myself, and God?

Ummmmmm . . . let's just say I'm working on it. Follow me on TikTok for updates! ☺

A SIMPLE PRAYER
FOR PERSPECTIVE

———

If this is not what it seems . . .
what is it?

Show me the opportunities for
growth that are hidden by pride.

Reveal to me the aching hearts
hidden by the pride of others.

Build in me the gratitude that
requires me to celebrate myself.

EXISTENTIAL COLOR SCHEME

TEAL
is the new black

BLACK
is the new pink

PINK
is the new bold

BOLD
is the new think

THINK
is the old know

KNOW
is the new knew

KNEW
is the old faith

FAITH
is the new you

Just a Minute

MANNA MEDITATION

In Exodus 16, Moses told a story about how God fed his people bread from heaven as they wandered in the desert.

- Set a timer for 60 seconds.

- Inhale through your nose, exhale through your mouth.

- Cup your hands, creating a bowl in front of you.

- Allow your thoughts to rest on the words *Give us this day our daily bread.*

- Visualizing a warm loaf of fresh, fragrant bread in your hands, receive it as a symbol of God's care for you. The daily bread Jesus spoke of in the Lord's Prayer—the manna that came to God's people in the desert—is baked fresh for you exactly when you need it.

Doodle Time

DRAW A LINE FROM THE MOMENT TO THE EMOTICON.

First cup of coffee

Cooking dinner

Climbing stairs

Making small talk with strangers

Traffic

Falling asleep last night

Last time you talked to your mom

Any given workday

Most recent WTF moment

Snuggling with my pup, Thunder

TS ABOUT
VERTIGO

I wake up on a lopsided planet, the floor pitching and tilting beneath my feet. Walls swim. The ceiling over my head is spinning like the blades of a helicopter. I feel myself free-falling.

WELCOME TO MY
vertigo
vertigo
vertigo
vertigo
vertigo
vertigo
vertigo

I prop myself up, eyes closed. "Joshy?"

My boyfriend recognizes the seasickness in my voice.

"Oh, babe," he says, because sometimes the best thing you can say to someone is "oh, babe" in that way —

woops! gotta barf

I weave my way to the barfatorium and when I feel a little better, I weave my way back to bed. It's been years since I was diagnosed with Ménière's. How many years? So many years with Ménière's

disease, an inner-ear disturbance that causes vertigo, cluster headaches (and cluster you-know-whats), ringing in the ears, unbearable fullness, and other ear-centric calamity.

The first time I woke up to the spinning reality of Ménière's, I was a happy little New Yorker in my twenties. By day, I was rehearsing *Steel Pier*, a musical about a dance marathon. By night, I was performing in *Scapin*, a slapstick adaptation of a French neoclassic by Molière. I was thrilled to be singing and dancing, eating at Cafe Lalo, tossing around phrases like "French neoclassic" and "paycheck." I was living the dream of every aspiring actor in New York.

Until I woke up on a tilt-o-whirl. I've learned everything I can about this thing that would be my archnemesis, my kryptonite. I've studied it. Tried to make sense of it. I've never gotten used to the drunken compass or the debilitating symptoms.

ALL I CAN DO IS DEVELOP MY OWN ... velop mo ...

Oh, Babe
gotta
barf

All I can do is develop my own coping mechanisms.

I know how to stack the pillows without turning my head. I know which brand of saltines to have on hand. I know how to swiftly twist my hair into a scrunchy before I throw up. I practice box breathing—or out-of-the-box breathing.

INHALE 2 · 3 · 4
HOLD 2 · 3 · 4
EXHALE 2 · 3 · 4
HOLD 2 · 3 · 4
INHALE 2 · 3 · 4

We all have our coping mechanisms.

I know all about the magical kingdom deep inside my ear. I protect those two little fairy caves on either side of my head. I shnoozle them with earmuffs and flap hats. I made it my business to learn about the tiny bones—the ossicles: malleus, incus, and stapes—to whom God gave an unimaginable superpower. They can transform the slightest movement of the air into sound. Malleus, incus, and stapes are my angels of music; I have perfect pitch, and I treasure that gift. The only cure for Ménière's is inner ear surgery, and I can't risk it. I can't bear to think about waking up to a world without music. I'd rather wake up reeling. Or not wake up at all.

As my understanding of vertigo has evolved, so have my prayers.

In my twenties, I prayed, "Oh, God! Make it stop! Make it stop!"

In my thirties, I prayed, "God, help me muscle through this so I can do what I need to do."

And now, I pray, "God, set your hand on those who need something from me today. Be there for them in all the ways I can't. Give me the strength to make way for the strength of others. Grant me the grace to be what you want me to be—even if that means being quiet."

And then I say a prayer of thanks for Josh, who comes and goes without advice or pity, who doesn't try to tell me I can overcome this if I have a positive attitude, who is simply there with me in my swirling universe.

i suspect YOUR world like mine at times tilts and whirls.

There are so many kinds of personal vertigo. So many dynamics—internal and external—just waiting to spin us out and disorient us. So many awakenings that humble and rearrange us.

Today my vertigo is made of Ménière's.

There have been other days when depression, anxiety, or the hard fact of being overextended cause a spinout. And there are days when I know someone close to me is spinning out, and there's not a damn thing I can do to help them. They'll have to make their own difficult choices and employ whatever coping mechanisms work for them.

The one thing we know for a fact is that no one gets through life perfectly in place like a bubble at the center of a carpenter's level. Who would even want that? Knowing that we will at some point need to access that core of stability, it's probably a good idea to set a few safety measures in place. For example:

Cultivating a circle of love in which we know others will be there for us because we've been there for them.

Developing a practice of establishing firm boundaries and a vocabulary of gentle language that helps us maintain them.

Committing ourselves to a lifestyle of self-care.

Perhaps the hardest aspect of regaining equilibrium is letting go of the idea that your momentary imbalance is a symptom of inadequacy or a sign that you're outside God's favor.

During a particularly low moment, I wrote in my journal:

There are great words to describe the emptiness
and devastation of the sacrifices I've made.
I'm not sure it's been worth it.

Oh God, don't let me leave without a song in my heart.

You put it there first before I came here.

I don't want to leave without one.

At least one.

"Out of the depths I cry to you, LORD," David wrote in Psalm 130. "I wait for the LORD, my whole being waits, and in his word I put my hope" (NIV).

These words come from a portion of Hebrew scripture called "The Song of Ascents"—probably because they were sung as worshippers climbed hills and staircases leading to the temple. That had to be a hard slog, but the psalms are overwhelmingly hopeful.

"I put my hope," said David.

My hope.

It is mine to set in motion or place, still and solid.

I know I'll sleep eventually and wake up with fresh reverence for the rocking and reeling of this crazy world.

*I am at the center
of a tightrope.*

*Be the muscle
that strengthens my
outstretched arms.*

Just breathe

INHALE SIMPLICITY

exhale clutter

INHALE ASSURANCE

exhale apprehension

INHALE GRATITUDE

exhale lassitude

INHALE RESILIENCE

exhale doubt

Mood Vertigo

(Sing to the tune of Duke Ellington's "Mood Indigo.")

I can't stand up, no, no, no
I can't stand up
'Cause I got that mood vertigo
That feelin' goes stealin' from my head to my heel
While I regurgitate my last meal.
Always get that mood vertigo
Down deep inside my cochlea
In the mornin' when I feel low
I'm overwhelmed with nausea.
'Cause no one really knows how to help me
When I wake up reeling and I gotta pee
When I get that mood vertigo
I could lay me down and cry.

WORDS AND PHRASES I CAN'T SAY BECAUSE THEY GROSS ME OUT

- HOT SUBWAY URINE
- CRAPBALLS
- MOIST
- PUKE
- PUCE (LOVE THE COLOR, HATE THE WORD, WHICH SOUNDS LIKE PUKE)
- CERVICAL SPINE
- STEROIDS

- POLITICS
- "AT THE END OF THE DAY . . . "
- "LET'S PIVOT"
- MEALY
- KNEECAPPED
- TRUMP
- "PICK YOUR BRAIN"
- "HONOR JUST TO BE NOMINATED"

Better Angels
BRACKET

GRUDGE-MONGER

GET OVER IT

GET OVER IT

OBLIGATION

GENEROSITY

GENEROSITY

GENEROSITY

GENEROSITY

TOLERANCE

ACCEPTANCE

ACCEPTANCE

LOVE

SELF-RIGHTEOUSNESS

LOVE

LOVE

LOVE

PARTIAL LIST OF THINGS THAT MIGHT MAKE YOU FEEL BETTER RIGHT NOW

- KRISPY KREME DOUGHNUTS
- HUGGING A GOOD DOG
- HUGGING A GOOD PERSON
- SOUP
- THE SMELL OF YOUR MOM'S HOUSE
- LADYBUG LANDING ON YOUR SLEEVE
- BLOWING DANDELION FEATHERS

- CHAMOMILE TEA WITH HONEY
- THREE DEEP BREATHS
- HOT BATH
- ICE PACK
- HEATING PAD
- SMILING AT A FRIEND
- SMILING AT A STRANGER
- SAYING A LITTLE PRAYER

Playlist for a Life Gone Sideways

Dr. Jacob Jolij, a cognitive neuroscientist, developed a formula for discerning the most uplifting songs for the human brain, based on lyrics with a positive message, variations from major keys, chord progressions, and beats per minute. Based on that criteria, I've developed this mega-uplifting playlist. You're welcome.

"OH HAPPY DAY"
EDWIN HAWKINS SINGERS

"WALKING ON SUNSHINE"
KATRINA AND THE WAVES

"HEROES"
DAVID BOWIE

"HAIL HOLY QUEEN"
NUNS IN *SISTER ACT*

"BACK IN BABY'S ARMS"
PATSY CLINE

"9 TO 5"
DOLLY PARTON

"RASPBERRY BERET"
PRINCE

"FREE"
ULTRA NATÉ

"I WILL SURVIVE"
GLORIA GAYNOR

"UNWRITTEN"
NATASHA BEDINGFIELD

"NO TEARS LEFT TO CRY"
ARIANA GRANDE

THOUGH

TS ABOUT
OPENNESS

I've always loved that moment in Mark chapter 7 when Jesus touched the ear of a deaf man and said, "*Ephphatha!*" It means, "Be opened." Suddenly, this man, deaf from birth, could hear, and his immediate response was to sing.

Ponder with me for a moment the concept of *openness* as a transition from silence to singing.

Florence Birdwell at Oklahoma City University taught me to sing. Not just vocalize. Really *sing* from my gut, from my soul, from somewhere deep down in my hoo-hoo. This was not an easy process, because nobody's gonna teach you a dang thing until you're open to learn. This requires a leap of faith,

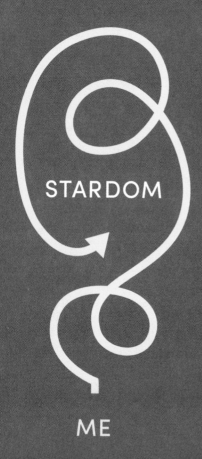

STARDOM

ME

MY
PLAN

WISDOM

ME

GOD'S
PLAN

an act of courage, and I was a kid when Flo Bird came into my life. I didn't have a clue about the level of discipline it would take to achieve what she believed I was capable of achieving.

Luckily, *opening* was her gift.

She opened my throat, opened my lungs, opened my eyes. She opened doors and windows in my soul.

I graduated from OCU with a master's degree and got a full-ride scholarship to the prestigious Academy of Vocal Arts in Philadelphia, but on my way there, I detoured to visit friends in New York and ended up on Broadway. That's the drastically abbreviated version. We don't have time for the *Lord of the Rings* saga that actually details the convoluted life of me or anyone else who's ever worked in show business. Suffice it to say: I did well.

For a long time, I continued on my busy way, operating with a set of standards and practices that, by and large, worked out

> Nobody's gonna teach you a dang thing until you're open to learn.

really well for me. You know how that goes. You maintain your baseline happiness—or at least a baseline comfort zone. You get in the habit of protecting that comfort zone, because that comfort zone protects you.

We all tend to see ourselves in a pretty specific context, and anything outside that setting makes you feel like you got your shoes on the wrong feet. Opening yourself to a new way of thinking—making yourself available to a context you can't control—means dropping that old arsenal of defense mechanisms, and that's scary.

But then something kinda major happened—a literal and metaphorical kick in the head—and I'll tell you about that in a minute, but the point is: I stopped. I listened. I plugged into a newly electrified current of awareness. I'm not sure it was even a choice. In retrospect, it seems like a God thing, because a lot of stuff started happening for me, professionally and personally. I opened myself to a different context and started singing a whole new song.

Now, here's a little heads-up: opening swings both ways—incoming and outgoing. Be prepared for a tornado of emotions that shouldn't be able to coexist.

Fragility and strength.

Shame and pride.

Love and anger.

Doubt and faith.

It's like that old Cole Porter song in *Kiss Me, Kate*—"Another Op'nin', Another Show"—that has everybody waxing enthusiastic about the simultaneously thrilling and terrifying possibilities, fully recognizing that any big show is "another pain where the ulcers grow" and a job with the potential to "make your future forget your past." You might soar and learn;

you might crash and burn. Cole Porter's wise advice: "Cross your fingers and hold your heart."

Opening a show is literally a revelation; you reveal your work to the audience, and the work reveals a new edition of you to yourself. Being open exposes you to both criticism and applause, rotten tomatoes or a standing ovation, but more important, it sweeps you forward from everything that was into everything that can be. All the planning and preparation in the world doesn't guarantee a good outcome.

Broadway is a risky business. So is life.

That's probably why so many people prefer to stay closed. And that's okay.

I can make a strong case for "leap and a net will appear," but no one should ever be shamed or cajoled into taking a risk that doesn't feel right for them in their current headspace. Sometimes our guts tell us to stop, check ourselves, and proceed with caution. And it's dangerous to ignore your gut.

So how do you know when it's your moment?

You know.

Being open exposes you to both criticism and applause, rotten tomatoes or a standing ovation, but more important, it sweeps you forward from everything that was into everything that can be.

Broadway is a risky business. *So is life.*

You summon up all your self-honesty, separate caution from fear, and listen for the answer already within you.

Remember in the book of 1 Kings how Elijah stood on the mountain, listening for an answer?

First came a mighty wind—almost as loud as the buzzing of the Twitter hive mind—but God wasn't in the noise.

Then came an earthquake—kinda like, oh, let's see . . . a pandemic, maybe? But God wasn't in the chaos.

Then came a firestorm. [Insert the natural disaster of your choice.] But God wasn't in the scorched earth.

And then came a whisper—a "still, small voice"—that asked, "What are you doing here?"

I love that God came to Elijah with a question instead of an answer, and I love this particular question as an opening.

What are you doing here?

Are you happy?

Are you helping?

Right here, right now: Are you lying to yourself or telling the truth? Are you living your best life or a life someone else designed for you?

You know.

You wait in the wings, breathing in the dark, listening for the overture, and when it's time, you step into the light.

A SIMPLE PRAYER
FOR STARTING OVER

Oh, Lord, help me get:

- *Off my butt*

- *On my feet*

- *Over myself*

WHO SAID IT BEST?

Roman philosopher Seneca

"Every new beginning comes from some other beginning's end."

The Dakota Ramblers

"Shut the door, I'm comin' in the window."

Open Wide

INHALE THROUGH YOUR NOSE,
exhale through your mouth.

- Start with your arms crossed, giving yourself a hug.
- Allowing your thoughts to rest on the word *open*, slowly open your arms until they're stretched out in front of you and then out to the sides as far as you can in both directions.

Now use this space to answer the question:

What are you doing here?

APPLY AS NEEDED TO LIFE AND CANCEL CULTURE

Keep an open mind.
But not so open that
your brains fall out.

WALTER KOTSCHNIG
(paraphrased)

Rise! Shine!
Give God the glory!
Also try to eat some protein.
Or just screw it and
watch Netflix.
There's always tomorrow . . .

Randomania

Know what the Zen master
said to the hot dog vendor?

"Make me one with everything."

TS ABOUT
NNECTION

After I shared some thoughts about my adoption in my memoir, *A Little Bit Wicked, The Oprah Winfrey Show* reached out and asked me if I'd be willing to come on the show and be reunited with my birth mother. They said she could be found by a fella named Troy Dunn. They called him The Locator.

How is that not a reality show right now? Every week, between *Maltese Moms* (my idea for a reality show about the rigors of caring for a dog who has more contract riders than Little Richard) and *Growing Up Ghastly* (my idea for a reality show about families who live next to cemeteries), The Locator would track down a person who's made very plain their wishes to remain unfound.

That was a hard pass for me. I adore Oprah, and I knew her staff had the best of intentions, but it just didn't feel like the right time nor place. Don't get me wrong: I had questions. I'm a curious little Nancy Drew when it comes to everyday mysteries.

How many blueberries in a cup?

Am I getting enough riboflavin?

What's the secret in the secret sauce?

Of course, I had questions! But maybe not the ones you think.

I never wanted to ask my bio mom, "Why didn't you keep me?" I wanted to ask her, "Where did you find the strength to let me go?"

Whoever this woman was, she went through the pain and effort of bringing me into the world, and then she had the humility and grace to recognize that I belonged to someone else. She placed me in a closed adoption, retaining her anonymity. I was happy to respect her wishes. I had no desire to disrupt her life or peek inside some unpredictable can of worms that might disrupt my own.

Connection feels risky, because it is. You can't always let your heart rule your head. You feel your way forward, for the right reasons and at your own pace. There's a sweet spot somewhere between "fools rush in" and "f#ck all y'all." Only you know where and when that is. No one has the right to pressure you to make a connection you're not ready for.

Overwhelmingly, my feeling toward my biological mother was gratitude, and I thought it was important to honor that feeling, so every year on my birthday, I checked into a nice hotel and spent a good part of the day focusing prayers, thanks, and good energy on her, hoping she'd feel my love and gratitude, wherever she might be. I was open to the idea that she wanted that door closed, but I always kept an open door for her in my heart. It didn't matter to me if she could feel the breeze passing through that open door.

I felt it.

So here's where it gets into the mystic:

Years after I turned down that offer from the Oprah show, I was in a place where I finally did feel ready to take the next step, but I wasn't sure how to go about it. Out of the blue, I got a call from The Locator. That fella Troy Dunn called me up and said, "I felt like it was laid on my heart to reach out. I have some information about your birth mother if you're open to it."

"Yes," I said. "I'm open."

A few months later, I met Mama Lynn. As we chattered and cried and caught up on forty-some years of separate destinies, she told me, "Every year on your birthday, I found a room where I could be by myself and pray for you, hoping you'd feel my love."

Connection.

It's happening, all around you, all the time, in ways you can't see or hear or even imagine. Plug in, pay attention, and be patient with yourself. Connection is there for you when you're ready.

> Plug in, pay attention, and be patient with yourself. Connection is there for you when you're ready.

I'd bet dollars to doughnuts, someone needs someone exactly like you and they're preparing to welcome you into their life. I suspect someone misses you and listens for your footsteps on the stairs. Someone remembers the corner of your smile and laughs out loud when they think of that time y'all two were at the whatchamacallit. Someone knows you exist and cares that you're happy, and all those *someones* connect you to the great *everyone*.

This I can promise: If you find a quiet place to close your eyes and let yourself feel it, someone will be praying for you.

SPOILER ALERT: It's me.

Timeless Text Messages

Kristin

Mama Lynn, you made the wonderful decision that gave me life. Thank you.

Kristin

Mom, you made the wonderful decision that gave me a life. Thank you.

*In your all-encompassing
arms, let me be encompassed.*

*In your all-seeing eye,
let me be seen.*

*In the eternity of this moment,
let me be fully present.*

FRIENDLY REMINDER

There's a difference between

individualism and selfishness.

Jesus was a rugged individualist,

and he cared about other people.

Be an individualist like Jesus.

Write the love letter you need to receive.

1 Use this space to write a note of encouragement.

2 Sign the note "someone who loves you."

3 Tear it out and tuck it in the pocket of a coat you won't wear for a while.

*Remember that time when
you thought I forgot about you?*

I DIDN'T.

THOUGH

TS ABOUT
LOVING

The *Wizard of Oz* gave us many pearls of wisdom, including "There's no place like home," but there's a pivotal snippet of dialogue with which I must take issue. Remember that moment in the movie when the so-called wizard is bestowing charming but totally disingenuous gifts on the Scarecrow, the Tin Man, and the Cowardly Lion?

First off, a diploma makes you smart? I know so many people who disprove that theory in both directions.

SO. MANY. PEOPLE.

A medal makes you a hero? Teachers, single moms, and nurses debunk that one about eight billion times a day.

But it's the next one that gets me out of my chair.

The Wizard says to the Tin Man: "Remember, my sentimental friend, that a heart is not judged by how much you love, but by how much you are loved by others."

Excuse me? In a flying monkey's butt, it does! "How much you are loved by others"—according to what metric? Likes? Shares? Right swipes? That's how you measure popularity. Trust me. I know all about popular. After a few decades in Hollywood, it's not hard to tell the difference between popularity and love.

Being "loved by others" is easy. Babies do it between mashed bananas and naptime. Fish do it while swimming in their own toilet. I have several pairs of shoes that get a lot of love from me and give me nothing but torment in return. But "how much you love" is a choice. It's hard work sometimes, and if you're doing love right, it takes brains, courage, and heart all at once.

"How much you are loved by others" ebbs and flows according to a lot of external factors. "How much you love" is the constant North Star that steers everything you do.

Your love has value, no matter how other people choose to respond to it. If you love someone who doesn't love you back, your love is still a force of nature. Your love changes and strengthens you and opens your heart to love again.

If you love someone who dies, your love keeps their spirit

THE
greatest thing
YOU'LL EVER LEARN
is just to love
AND BE
loved in return.

EDEN AHBEZ

alive. Your love is their legacy—their story written on your heart. Long after they're gone, their song echoes through you.

If you devote your life to loving others—serving strangers, most of whom will never know or thank you—your love has the power to change the world. If you love only those who are lovable, honey, you're a love amateur. If you choose love while others choose hate, that's some bravura *hey, Romeo, hold my beer* master's-level love.

The way you love people is not about who they are; it's about who *you* are. And the way other people love or don't love you, honey—do the math. That's about them. If you live within the architecture of love—tenderness for the people close to you, compassion for strangers, generosity toward your less-than-best self—you'll be living a richer, fuller, more joyful life.

Love that aches, love that heals, love that makes the world go around—it's all good. So just you keep on loving, you lovely little love muffin, even in those moments when you don't feel love coming back to you.

Love anyway.

Love without reserve or regret.

Dwell in love. Personify love.

Pay no attention to that man behind the curtain.

*I know
love is real.*

*Help me
prove it.*

*Make me
an instrument.*

*Tune me up
and play me.*

*Let me be part of the flash-mob
symphony of love that's out there,
just waiting to happen.*

LOVE CHAPTER CHECKLIST

HOW ARE YOU DOING ON 1 CORINTHIANS 13?

Love is . . .

	NAILED IT	NEEDS WORK
Patient	☐	☐
Kind	☐	☐
Not envious	☐	☐
Not stuck-up	☐	☐
Not rude	☐	☐
Slow to anger	☐	☐
Forgiving	☐	☐
Resistant to BS	☐	☐
Rejoicing in truth	☐	☐
Protective	☐	☐
Trusting	☐	☐
Optimistic	☐	☐
Persevering	☐	☐
Unfailing	☐	☐

*Live in fragments
no longer.*

E.M. FORSTER

Didn't you hear me say
the first time I said,
"You are fabulous"?
Okay, fine.
I'll keep repeating it.
YOU ARE FABULOUS.
YOU ARE FABULOUS.
YOU ARE FABULOUS.

A SHORT LIST OF THINGS I CAN'T/WON'T SHUT UP ABOUT

- MUSIC

- MY FAITH

- BROADWAY CARES

- THE NEED FOR MORE WOMEN BEHIND THE CAMERA

- THE IMPORTANCE OF BEING A GOOD TIPPER

- PET ADOPTION

- BALMAIN JACKET ½ OFF OF ½ OFF!

PARTIAL LIST OF PEOPLE WHO PROBABLY NEED MY LOVE RIGHT NOW

- ANYONE WHO LIVES WITH ME
- ANYONE WHO LIVES WITH AN @$$HOLE
- ANYONE WHO IS AN @$$HOLE
- FOLKS WHO WORK AT ANIMAL SHELTERS
- FOLKS WHO GET NERVOUS ABOUT TRAVELING
- CAREGIVERS
- TIFFANY TRUMP
- PEOPLE IN LINE AT THE DMV
- PEOPLE IN LINE AT THE DMV WITH TIFFANY TRUMP

ZEN VENN *Rock of Ages*

WAYS THE ROCK OF GIBRALTAR IS SUPPORTIVE

WAYS GOD IS SUPPORTIVE

PROVIDING A HOME FOR HILARIOUS LITTLE MONKEYS

ROCK SOLID

MIRACLES

JUST BEING THERE

NO JUDGMENT

PROVIDING WINE

LENDING ME YOUR PINK LOUBOUTINS

WAYS YOU CAN BE SUPPORTIVE

THOUGH

TS ABOUT
WORK

Mama Lynn was no angel, but she had wings. Until a few years ago, the only scrap of information I had about my biological mother was that she had been a flight attendant. But that's actually a lot if you think about it. A whole story unfurls when you consider what it meant to be a flight attendant—excuse me, steward*ess*, as she prefers—before the dawn of Gloria Steinem.

The fact that she was a "Braniff Girl" takes it to a whole 'nother level.

Braniff was the Broadway of airlines: chic, showy, and full of celebrities. In 1968, the year I was born, Braniff launched an ad campaign with the slogan "When you got it, flaunt it." Magazine ads and TV commercials featured Salvador Dalí, Andy Warhol, Sonny Liston, and an elite squad of gorgeous Braniff Girls wearing uniforms designed by Italian fashion icon Emilio Pucci. They came in a variety of figure-flattering styles, psychedelic prints, and bold color blocking, with the option of a clear Lucite helmet—the Rain Dome—that protected beehive hairdos from cruel weather elements as the "air hostess" dashed in high-heeled go-go boots across the tarmac from the terminal to the airplane stairs.

To be a Braniff Girl, you had to be smart, slender, pageant-caliber beautiful, and willing to go anywhere. The job required a performative flair: the ability to read a room, think on your feet, and improvise as needed. In a world that offered slim opportunities for working women, a Braniff Girl could achieve financial freedom while living a life of grand adventure. But it could also be a life of difficult choices. A lonely life at times.

Even when I had only that single scrap of biographical data about my mother, I felt a thrill of understanding, because the life of a hardworking diva requires a similar skill set and comes with many of the same life choices and challenges, including a seemingly endless blur of boarding and deplaning one flight after another.

Like a Braniff Girl, a Broadway girl is vulnerable to hazards of high winds and the ecstasy that comes with defying gravity. Her resilience is constantly tested in the shadow of a ticking clock. The only thing she knows for sure is that what goes up must come down.

In the Stephen Sondheim musical *Company*—a really scrumptious mid-mod operetta—there's an elegantly simple song called "Barcelona," which takes place the morning after a randy bachelor, Bobby, gets lucky with April, a beautiful stewardess.

April is the very embodiment of getting lucky. I mean, she's a *stewardess*. Come on! In 1970 that was gold-standard lucky. But Bobby is a commitment-phobe who doesn't know what to do with his good fortune. We hear the unspoken questions of his aching heart in the music: *Who are you? What am I supposed to do now? Why are you leaving?*

But the best he can do out loud is, "Where ya going?"

"Barcelona," she sings. "Flight eighteen."

Bobby begs April to "put your wings down and stay."

"Barcelona," she sings. "And Madrid."

She has to go. This is her life. Her vocation. Everything she's worked incredibly hard to achieve, even if he clearly doesn't get how important that is to her, even though the whole world, including Stephen Sondheim, is constantly telling her that what she really should want is a man. In the show, that moment is an awakening. In my mother's life, that moment was me.

I can't pretend to know what that choice was like for her. The closest I've come to parenting is that time I Ambien-tweeted something about adopting a child from Cofevestan. By the time I woke up the next day, all the tabloids had jumped on it.

Oh! Here's another Ambien tweet fiasco: I was watching a true crime show about a newlywed couple on a cruise ship—the groom had pushed the bride overboard, I think—and I tweeted something like, "Don't go on a cruise, especially if you're a newlywed. One of you won't come back!"

Thunk. Zzzzzzzzzzz . . .

The next day, I woke up to a blizzard of "WTF?!" text messages and emails—my manager, my lawyer, my agent—reminding me that I had recently signed an endorsement deal with Royal Caribbean. I was supposed to christen their luxurious new cruise ship, and now they were talking about firing me. I had no memory of the Ambien tweet, so it was like, "What? Why? Whoa . . ."

Moral of the story: like a stewardess on a red-eye, a diva never sleeps. Being Kristin Chenoweth is what I do, and I don't get to take the night off. Some jobs are defined as "I work at bibbety bobbety boo," and some jobs are defined as "I *am* a bibbety bobbety boo."

I don't work at Hollywood; I am a performer.

My mom didn't work at nursing; she was a nurse.

PROBABILITY THAT EVERYTHING WILL GO AS PLANNED

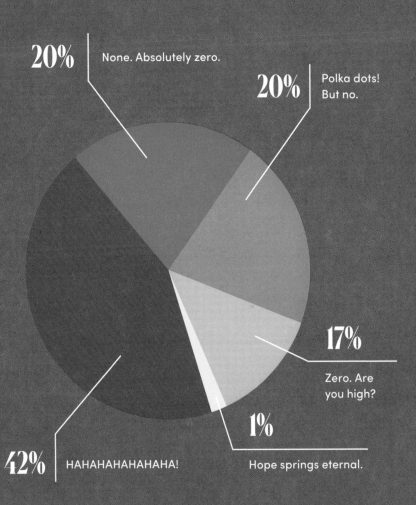

20% None. Absolutely zero.

20% Polka dots! But no.

17% Zero. Are you high?

1% Hope springs eternal.

42% HAHAHAHAHAHAHA!

Another word for vocation is *calling*. Were you hired to do your job, or were you called? Either way, you will sacrifice something—time, energy, a chunk of your life—to do that work. It's not realistic to think that you'll get through your whole life without feeling the burn of that sacrifice. In some waking or sleeping dreamscape, you'll see another path that might have been, and that can mess with your head. All you can do in that moment is listen.

Do you still hear the calling?

It scares me a little, but I want to share something I wrote in my journal during a dark moment after I was injured on *The Good Wife* set:

I hate everyone.

Mostly me.

My thoughts escape me, as I feel ready for the rapture.

I am my only friend. Everyone is paid or scattered.

My best friends don't know me anymore.

I don't even know myself.

That's the one thing I used to have that no one could have.

This business is killing me, yet I've given up everything for it.

I don't even know how to do anything else. If I could, and be happy, I would.

God, hear me. Please.

I might be done.

When the thoroughbred can't deliver anymore or cross the finish line—where do I go?

Where. Do. I. Go.

Tell me, and I will go. And I won't look back.

I suspect there are a lot of hardworking women in the entertainment industry—in any industry—who've detoured down that dark emotional alley. But it's weirdly reassuring in retrospect. When I was at the lowest low, my deepest fear was that I might not be able to work again, and that means I chose wisely when I dedicated my life to music and my work.

This world isn't built for single women who dedicate themselves to their work.

Oh, wait. I take it back.

Nuns.

Nuns are allowed to stay single, dedicate themselves to education and vocation and not be seated at the children's table at Thanksgiving. Nobody winks at a nun and says, "Oh, I think you'll change your mind and want a baby when you get older." No one expects a nun to invest in a closet full of single-use bridesmaid dresses. Nuns are all about the work, and they don't give a wimple if someone else doesn't understand or respect their life choices.

The movie *Holidate* is an irreverent exploration of that dynamic and the lengths women go to in an attempt to

BROADWAY SHOW

THE GOOD, THE BAD, AND THE GLITTERY

A FUNNY THING HAPPENED ON THE WAY TO THE EMERGENCY ROOM

GUARDIAN ANGELS IN AMERICA

CATS

CRAMALOT

DOLLY MADE ME DO IT

HOW TO SUCCEED IN BUSINESS WITHOUT REALLY FLYING

IN THE TIGHTS

avoid it. I played Aunt Susan, an F-bomb-dropping party girl who arranges a placeholder guy for compulsory holiday events. It sounds jaded, but it gives her time and space to do what she wants to do, unencumbered by family pressure or romantic entanglement. This movie is such a romp—we weren't trying to be *Out of Africa*—but there is a larger conversation to be had about it. Aunt Susan's worldview was a pleasure for me to hang out with. She was a hoot and restored me to a place where I felt the joy of working again.

Every summer at my Broadway Bootcamp (BBC), I tell the kids, "If there's anything else you can do and still be happy, do it." Because this work is exceptionally hard, and the odds are so stacked against them, even though they are ridiculously talented.

But what are the odds of success if you feel called to do something and never give it a shot?

You're not gonna get the part if you never show up for the audition.

The toughest thing for me to witness is when a truly talented performer doesn't get the breaks they deserve. In true Broadway fashion, they keep showing up, but it's like watching someone bang their head against a brick wall.

I wish I could wave a magic wand.

Historically, we've had this deeply ingrained American notion about the evil of "quitting"—not being "a quitter"—and

I have a problem with that. Changing course is not the same as "quitting." Throughout our lives, we have to adjust for industry shifts and our own personal growth. That doesn't mean you're "quitting" the thing that wasn't working; that means you're using that experience to achieve your larger purpose.

Working at McDonald's is a job; feeding people is a purpose. (Okay, now I really want McDonald's. *Focus, Kristi, focus!*) Sometimes we get so fixated on the job, we forget about the purpose, and in this day and age, you can't afford to be myopic like that. We're living in an extraordinary moment when the world has had to reinvent itself. We've had to reinvent ourselves and redefine the very concept of *work*—hopefully within the realm of our greater purpose.

> Changing course is not the same as "quitting."

That gig on *The Good Wife* is not the first fabulous job I lost. Not the first time I found myself in the full-time occupation of dragging myself out of my despair. Purpose has always pulled me forward into the future.

Purpose is the life water; work is the vessel.

---

*Lord, walk beside me
and hold my hand.*

Or even just my pinkie.

*Show me the next box
on the flowchart.*

*Hold on to everything else
until I get there.*

Insomnia as Emoticons

12 AM

1 AM

2 AM

3 AM

4 AM

5 AM

6 AM

7 AM

WHO SAID IT BEST?

Frank Capra

"Don't compromise. Believe in yourself. Because only the valiant can create."

Jerry Chenoweth

"Just suck it up and do what you do."

THOUGH
DI

TS ABOUT
SRUPTION

JULY 11, 2012.

I remember the exact date because 7/11 was always the day you could get a free Cherry Coke Slurpee at the 7-Eleven on 4th and Broadway. I was planning to stop off after my second day of shooting a seven-episode arc on *The Good Wife*. Dream gig. I'd get to live in New York and do a top-flight TV show with a whole lot of wonderful people, having loads of fun and making gobs of money. I could not have been happier to be there.

The scene was out on the street. Just me, talking on the phone. I remember I had a prop BlackBerry in my hand. The director called out, "*Action*."

And then I woke up at Bellevue Hospital.

"Miss Chenoweth? Miss Chenoweth? Can you hear me?"

Someone was patting my hand. Someone else was gently blotting my face with a cool, damp cloth. My teeth felt like a picket fence. I couldn't open my right eye. Blood trickled down my neck, warm and sticky.

My teeth felt like a picket fence.

"Miss Chenoweth, there's been an accident."

My memories of the following three weeks are twisted like pretzels and shot full of holes. Mom and Dad were there, thank God. And my lawyer. Nurses and doctors came and went, speaking gibberish and showing me X-rays of some poor, broken person I didn't recognize. Bits and pieces from the day of the accident came back in flickers and flashes.

The interior of an ambulance.

"You fell," someone said.

I fell, my woozy brain echoed. *Stupid me.*

"No, you didn't fall," someone else told me at the hospital.

CBS released a statement that I was struck by "silks"—which sounds so *silky*, doesn't it? Like a silk curtain wafted over me, and brittle little aphid that I am, I just somehow cracked into pieces like a Fabergé egg. In fact, I was standing on the street flanked by towering lighting equipment that included heavy screens called silks, which are supported by steel scaffolding. Just as the director called "Action!" the wind took a section that wasn't properly secured.

Picture a fly swatter coming at a gypsy moth.

It hit me full frontal and slammed me to the pavement. My head cracked against the curb, leaving a seven-inch gash that would have been worse, the doctor told me, if not for the tightly woven hair extensions that held my scalp together.

That's right. I owed what was left of my concussed brain to a well-placed line of hair extensions. Never—*never*—underestimate the power of a good weave.

That's some hard-won wisdom right there.

You're welcome.

In the weeks that followed, my swollen face looked like a bluish-purple catcher's mitt. My ribs seemed to shift like piano keys every time I inhaled. I was conscious of the shredded muscle fiber in my neck, the intricate pulley system you learn about as you refine vocal embouchure—the precise positioning of lips, jaw, tongue, teeth, cheekbones—all the extrinsic articulators that make it possible for me to sing the way I need to sing.

I struggled to think straight, struggled to talk right, struggled to get up in the morning. Painkillers muffled the persistent pounding headache, but my soul hurt. Depression descended, and I found myself cast in a grainy horror flick: *The Brokening*

We make plans.
God winks.

As we all know, when a horror flick gains traction, sequels follow, each with its own celebrity cameos and ominous theme music.

Brokening II: Headache from Hell

Brokening III: Journey to the Undertoilet (shot entirely on location in a hotel bathroom)

Brokening IV: Jason Returns (or *I Keep Calling My Assistant Jordan "Jason" on Account of My Head Is Brokened*)

Brokening V: Why, God, Why? (theme music by Lana Del Rey)

Brokening VI: Tell Me Again About My Positive Attitude, I F#@%ing Dare You (guest cameo by Alan Cumming)

This was a personal and professional setback of devastating proportions. I lost one of the sweetest gigs I'd ever had and felt abandoned by the people who were supposed to look out for me.

And, no, I did not get my Cherry Coke Slurpee.

I won't lie. I have some unresolved anger about it.

At first, I was mostly out of it, floating on a stagnant green swimming pool of painkillers. When I started to come out of it, I was seriously pissed. Rage is a crazy chemical cocktail: fear, loss, agony, frustration, and fight-or-flight adrenaline. It hijacks your face filter and squashes your immune system. I wanted to make peace with what had happened and forgive the people whose actions (or inactions) disappointed me, but you can't just flip a switch on all that. This ain't *Frozen*. You can't just let it go.

Honoring our anger is a necessary first step to forgiveness. Don't forget: Jesus got righteously pissed off on several occasions, and he let it be known. There's nothing virtuous about pretending you're above getting mad. Rage doesn't have to be a bully; rage can be a teacher and a tour guide, and it can leave you with the knowledge and the belly fire to be a hero for those who aren't able to stand up for themselves.

Honoring our anger is a necessary first step to forgiveness.

So, yeah, I was mad, and I'm still working through that, but I've been careful to keep that anger clean and contained. I've been thinking differently about the very real consequences that can happen in this industry that's all about make-believe.

Early in my career, I met Bette Midler at a party, and she said, "Hey, kid, how's show business?"

"Oh, it's wonderful!" I gushed, and I told her all about my Broadway thing and my TV thing and my movie thing and how lovely all the people are.

Bette laughed and said, "Okay."

She said it in this wiseass way that seemed so sideways to me at the time. Now I get it.

Boy, do I get it.

The women in this business blow me away. Not just the legends—like Bette, Dolly Parton, Carol Burnett—no, I mean the working girls in the chorus and orchestra pit, backstage, up in the rigging, down in the trenches. Women in this business are always trying to push envelopes. We've fought so hard for every opportunity. We're all so glad and grateful to be here, we'll do almost anything we're asked to do. And there are those who can and do take advantage of that.

I think about the people who've died on movie sets, and I'm grateful I wasn't killed, but since that moment—"*Action!*"—I have not known one day without pain, and there are days when that pain does define me.

That moment changed everything. It changed me.

I struggled through a long, dark valley of depression, but in the months and years that followed, something in my addled brain began to stir. I became aware of ideas and desires that surprised me. I let those ideas germinate. I allowed those desires to bubble to the surface. I gave time and space and oxygen to my own audacity—dreams and daring, ambition and saltiness—and exciting things began to happen. Maybe it was the way electrical pathways in my brain were rerouted by the concussion, or maybe it was just time for me to take notice of some things I'd been too busy to think about.

Either way, I felt it as God.

Not that God conked me on the head to get my attention! Not at all.

I don't see God in the silks.

I see God in my hair extensions.

There's a level of comfort we aspire to in life—a financial umbrella, a well-stuffed chair, people and dogs who love us—and when we get to that place, we're not excited to have our comfort disrupted. But the price of personal comfort is the sacrifice of personal growth. We don't feel the opportunities and ideas that slide off our laps when we're comfortably clothed in the silk pajama pants of complacency. No, that happens without us even realizing it.

> The price of personal comfort is the sacrifice of personal growth.

Disruption is abrupt—even unkind—and we feel it as a loss, because it is. It is a loss! We have to honor and mourn it, but then we gotta be honest with ourselves about what we were willing to sacrifice for the status quo.

I despise the phrase *new normal*.

That's no longer what I aspire to. I aspire to a new

*ab*normal—a new understanding that *normal* is an illusion every bit as faked up and overmarketed as diet soda and Skittles.

No offense, Skittles! I love you. I do! I will eat you all day and twice on Sunday, but titanium dioxide does not taste like a rainbow. Unicorns do not fart you. Why can't we be honest with each other and celebrate my attraction to the immutable aftertaste of your hydrogenated palm-kernel oil?

But I digress.

My point: Disruption is, pardon my French, a bitch.

But so am I, sometimes, and people who love me are not put off by it, and I trust God to point the whole mess toward blessing.

Where to?

What for?

Why not?

*Fill me with
enterprising energy.*

*Gift me with an appetite
for disruption.*

*Sharpen my sense
of what-if...*

Partial list of things Shakespeare made us laugh at

- BALDNESS

- BELCHING

- HALITOSIS

- FARTING

- FECES / URINATION, GENERAL SCATOLOGY

- INSANE / POWER-MAD RULERS

- CRANKY WOMEN (*always played by men, of course*)

- DEATH

- LOVE

- THE HUMAN CONDITION

- OURSELVES

(Remember when folks used to laugh at human foible?)

TOTALLY LEGIT *BAD DAY* GROCERY LIST

Band-Aids

Bourbon

Hairspray

Matches

Comedy/Tragedy

COMEDY IS TRAGEDY'S BEST HOPE OF GETTING OVER ITSELF.

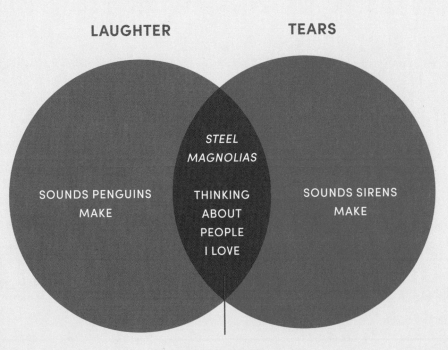

LAUGHTER   **TEARS**

STEEL MAGNOLIAS

THINKING ABOUT PEOPLE I LOVE

SOUNDS PENGUINS MAKE

SOUNDS SIRENS MAKE

LAUGHTER THROUGH TEARS

DEPRESSION

is a *F#@%ING*

LIAR.

Just a  Minute

CHAOS COPING MECHANISM

- Set a timer for 60 seconds.

- Inhale through your nose, exhale through your mouth.

- Allow your thoughts to rest on the word *hush*.

- Visualize a pond of croaking bullfrogs. As you hush them, they disappear beneath the calm surface of the water.

THOUGH

W

TS ABOUT
HAT FITS

Every article ever written about me mentions my size. I have a master's degree in opera. I've sold out Carnegie Hall. I've won Tony and Emmy awards. Somehow, even with all that on the table, they always feel the need to specifically note my height as four feet eleven or make oblique references to it with words like *elfin* or *teeny* or *minute*. I never get adjectives like *ballsy* or *robust*, no matter how hard I deliver that opening number or haul in that audience.

That never surprised me. I grew up in a world of "normal"-size people—if there is such a thing—but thank God, I was raised by a woman who had her own issues with fitting into

Troubleshooting 101

Draw a line between the problem and the solution.
Each solution may apply to multiple problems.

PROBLEM 😞

Bad romance

Computer issues

Wardrobe malfunction

Unfortunate haircut

Burned toast

Skin eruption

Parents driving you nuts

SOLUTION 😎

Duct tape

Safety pins

Call best friend

Cream of mushroom soup

Long nap

Box breathing exercise

Unplug and turn on again

*(Actually, now that I think of it, "long nap"
applies to most, if not all, of these.)*

a "normal"-size world. She brought me up with the understanding that fitting in is not all it's cracked up to be. As much as I struggle to put weight on, Mom struggles to take weight off. We share the same discombobulation with the fashion world; neither one of us travels the racks of the fours, sixes, and eights of this world. We dwell among the misfits at the outer edges where you learn to see things differently.

One of the perks of being in the public eye is that designers send you things for free, hoping you'll wear them and get seen. Of course, very little that gets sent to me comes in a size I can actually wear, but every once in a while I find something fun, and I love flashing it around so I can reward that designer and uplift another artist doing their craft.

A while back, I got a pile of cute clothes from a famous designer I was expected to sit next to at a Fashion Week luncheon. *Well, hello, Dolly!* To my delight, there was an adorable skirt that fit me perfectly. I paired that sweet little skirt with a statement tee and denim jacket, and if I do say so myself, I felt pretty adorable at that luncheon. I sat next to the designer and made sparkling conversation with everyone. But halfway through the salad, I kinda noticed that she had a look on her face like her parking meter needed plugging.

Long story short, the skirt was a tube top.

She didn't say anything about it, and by the time I found

out, I was like—hey, I've committed now. There's no going back. I'm just gonna rock my skirtubetop like it's the greatest invention since toaster waffles. If I'd let myself get all self-conscious and mortified about it, there would have been nowhere to hide. As it happens, the *New York Post* did use a picture of it, so she got some buzz out of it, for better or worse.

> You have to do what works for you, and that might mean disappointing or even upsetting people sometimes.

Brace yourself! Here comes the metaphor: People have all kinds of ideas about what they want you to do with the job opportunity, the suggestion, the conversation, the love—whatever it is they present to you. And bless their hearts. They are entitled to dream whatever dreams they like, but that doesn't equate to you being obligated to wear the costume and play the role in which they've cast you. You have to do what works for you, and that might mean disappointing or even upsetting people sometimes.

Now flip that script.

You are entitled to your vision of how your kid should use that education you provided. Or how your partner should use the time you've made available. Or how your friend should apply the advice you offered. Are you committed to that vision, or are you happy to see them apply their own instincts and rock it in a way that surprises you?

What fits us—who fits us, and when—these decisions are so personal and so subjective, it's dangerous to be swayed by opinions and agendas outside ourselves. It's hard to listen to the "still, small voice" inside when the rest of the world keeps shouting it down. "No, *this* is what your body is supposed to be. *This* is what your life is supposed to be. *This* is what everybody else is doing, so it must be right."

When the mainstream fits—great! Go with it. But if fitting in takes a lot of work—if it hogs your energy and robs you of your self-esteem—then I think you're better off keeping to that perimeter, hanging out with the irregulars, the home-made, and the not-for-everyone.

Find your fit. *Insist* on your fit.

Be willing to make alterations.

> It's hard to listen to the "still, small voice" inside when the rest of the world keeps shouting it down.

*Could we
please do this
some other
time?*

PARTIAL LIST OF THINGS
I TOTALLY BELIEVE IN

That's my story, and I'm sticking to it!

- SASQUATCH (THE TRUTH IS OUT THERE)

- FISH THAT GROW LEGS AND WALK OUT OF THE POND/LAKE/OCEAN

- MY DOG, THUNDER, SPEAKS ENGLISH

- LIFE ON OTHER PLANETS (IT'S SO BRASSY TO THINK ALL THIS IS JUST FOR US)

- YEARS OF BLEACHING MY ROOTS IS GOING TO MY BRAIN

- MY MOM HAS A PSYCHIC CONNECTION TO THOSE SHE LOVES MOST

- IMAGINARY FRIENDS WE HAVE AS CHILDREN ARE ANGELS HELPING US ALONG, AND WHEN WE GET OLDER, EVEN IF WE CAN'T SEE THEM ANYMORE, WE CAN STILL HEAR THEM; WE JUST HAVE TO LISTEN

- THE WRIGHT BROTHERS, WHO INVENTED FLIGHT, WERE TIME TRAVELERS AND CAME BACK TO DO US A SOLID

- TIME TRAVEL

- FATHER, SON, AND THE HOLY SPIRIT

- THE SECRET LIFE OF DRAGONFLIES

RSVP

I am otherwise engaged and will not be available for your outrage event.

ZEN VENN

Things I Believe In

THINGS I
CAN SEE

THINGS I
CAN'T SEE

THUNDER PUP
MOM AND DAD
BROADWAY

LOVE

WIND
SOUND WAVES
GOD
SASQUATCH

TS ABOUT
EWING UP

I sabelle Stevenson was a paragon: Tony Award doyenne, president of the American Theatre Wing, a pioneering performer, and lifelong advocate for those who make their life and living on the stage. Isabelle and I both received Tony Awards in 1999—mine was for *You're a Good Man, Charlie Brown* and hers was long-overdue recognition for lifetime achievement.

I was hoping we'd bump into each other again at the Tonys in 2003. I had just wrapped up a TV movie adaptation of *The Music Man* with Matthew Broderick and was about to open a little somethin' somethin' called *Wicked* on Broadway. Meanwhile, I had several other irons in the fire, including a sweet endorsement deal with Mrs. Beasley's. I was on fire! I had to get myself an assistant to field all the calls coming in.

So, one fine day, sorting through a flurry of messages, my assistant said to me, "Kristin, do you want to send something to this event honoring Isabelle Stevenson?" and I did. Of course! I wanted to join in the honoring. I had great admiration for Isabelle. Whatever this event was, I was certain she deserved it.

Cookies. Funeral. Scottish accent. Please. That's good TV.

As luck would have it, I had this cookie deal going, so—bam—no-brainer. I scrawled, "Congratulations, Isabelle! Love, Kristin Chenoweth" inside a card, stuck it in a great big ol' basket of cookies, and had the whole thing delivered to the event, which turned out to be . . .

Wait for it . . .

Isabelle's funeral.

My dear friend Alan Cumming loves to tell this story any time my name comes up in conversation—brunch, commuter flight, late-night talk show—and it's hilarious.

How is it not going to be hilarious?

Cookies. Funeral. Scottish accent. Please.

That's good TV. I get it.

And Isabelle did seem like the kind of person who would have found this hilarious herself. She was a vaudevillian. Before she became a mover/shaker in the world of New York theater, she toured with two guys as "Nice, Florio, & Lubow"—a dance act that featured her in a ballgown, them in top hats and tails, doing old-school physical comedy. Isabelle enjoyed a good pratfall.

So do I!

But this blunder was embarrassing to me as a young professional. It made me look clueless. My immaturity and self-involvement were on full display. It pained me to think about her family seeing that basket of cookies with its obvious backstory, and I didn't know if I'd be making it worse if I reached out to tell them I certainly meant no disrespect, that I was just too wrapped up in my impending stardom to hear about the death of a woman who'd blazed the trail for me.

So what may we extrapolate from this pratfall of a parable?

I suppose I learned something about vigilance, maybe? If I was slyer about this kind of thing, I'd spin it into something about celebrating the sweetness of life or some such bullcrap.

Alan's sensibilities are right on. It's a great anecdote that makes you laugh the same way you gotta laugh at a YouTube video of a pole dancer falling on her fanny or a pinstripe-suit executive tumbling down an escalator. The German word *schadenfreude* translates literally to something like "damage joy," but I don't think it's about taking malicious pleasure in someone else's misfortune. I think it reassures us to know that we're not taking that pratfall alone. It happens to everyone.

This, I'm afraid, is the moral of the story: everyone screws up. And that means you will screw up. I promise. Someday, somewhere, you will randomly embarrass yourself. You'll inadvertently do something hasty, thoughtless, or inappropriate, and there's nothing you can do to correct or cover it.

All you can do is *own it*.

The funeral cookies faux pas (which autocorrect keeps trying to change to "fox paws") wouldn't happen in the age of Twitter, because everybody knows everybody's business without waiting for *Page Six* or the *Times* obituaries, but social media offers much more spectacular opportunities for us all to embarrass ourselves and houses a whole kennel full of junkyard dogs who are just slobbering for somebody to screw up. If you fail—even for a second—to take ownership of a mistake, they get their teeth in your ankle, and they won't let go.

All you can
do is *own it*.

There is no outrage like internet outrage. It burns with the acid reflux of a million unrequited prom invitations. It's a hive of murder bees lying in wait for Winnie the Pooh.

After my concussion, I woke up.

There was an awakening.

I saw the world differently. I'm aware now in a way I wasn't before. I'm questioning my beliefs and searching my soul, but I'm not spending a lot of time or energy cringing about mistakes I made when I was less wise but every bit as well-intentioned. Every little fox paw in my past was part of an education that will continue as long as I'm open to it.

I've come far enough to know I have a long way to go, but I don't want to get canceled while I'm learning, and I don't want to leave my Christian sisters behind. I have faith in those good souls with their casseroles and Vacation Bible School. There are some wrong (IMHO) ideas deeply rooted in Southern Christianity, but I have to believe love will eventually triumph over them. I'm not willing to join the pile-on when someone's being canceled. It bothers me when the rhetoric of cancellation rhymes so closely with homophobia and other self-righteous excuses people come up with to hate on each other. When I disagree with someone, I'll speak

> I've come far enough to know I have a long way to go.

my heart to their heart privately and champion my beliefs in public, but cancellation is a form of hate, and I'm just not about that.

The only antivenom for cancellation is accountability.

Own. It.

If you've hurt someone, *own it*. Apologize. Try to make amends. If all you did was embarrass yourself, praise God and repeat after me: "There is zero net gain in beating myself up."

Don't let your embarrassment morph into self-loathing, self-doubt, or self-recrimination. Don't allow haters to paint any of that on you, and when someone else screws up, keep in mind the most dangerous words ever spoken by those who profess to love God: "Forgive us our trespasses as we forgive those who trespass against us" (Matthew 6:12, paraphrased).

It's not my job to tell other people they shouldn't be mad; the task before me is to own my mistakes, seek to understand the mistakes made by others, and be a purveyor of peace wherever I can.

When we screw up, what's left behind is a hilarious story, a lesson learned, or an emotional scar.

Guess which one plays best on late-night talk shows.

Forgive us our trespasses *as we forgive those who* trespass against us.

MATTHEW 6:12, PARAPHRASED

A SIMPLE PRAYER
FOR A STUPID MISTAKE

Ugh.

Give me grace to play the occasional role of punch line.

Help me sell myself on the value of a lesson learned.

Open my mouth to say, "I'm sorry," and shut my mouth before I say, "but..."

Forgive me my pratfalls as I forgive those who pratfall before me.

ASKING FOR A FRIEND

Is it rude to throw a strawberry cupcake in someone's mouth while they're talking?

Just a Minute

LET IT GO

- Set a timer for 60 seconds.

- Inhale through your nose, exhale through your mouth.

- With each breath, shrug your shoulders, slowly bringing them up, then letting them relax.

- Allow your thoughts to rest on the word *whatever*.

Come, come,
whoever you are,
wanderer, worshipper,
lover of leaving—
it doesn't matter.
*Ours is not a caravan
of despair.*

Rumi

THOUGH

TS ABOUT HARMONY

The first thing you hear on the Backroad Anthem sizzle reel is a span of masculine voices in tight harmony. And then the crowd goes berserk.

Josh and five of his friends began making music together in church in 2012 and quickly realized they had something special. They started touring, selling out college town venues, opening for national artists—Dustin Lynch, Eli Young Band, Lynyrd Skynyrd—doing all the nitty-gritty things a band has to do on an upward trajectory. As they bonded and became best friends, the band brothers exuded a joyfully goofy vibe, and the harmony took on the sort of integrity that usually happens only in family bands. There was love in it.

In December 2015, Backroad Anthem was the epitome of *almost there*; they'd just dropped an EP that was getting a lot of buzz and were poised to roll out a video. They were booked to headline a show in Little Rock on New Year's Eve but spent Christmas at home. The band's twenty-nine-year-old front man, Craig Strickland, went out duck hunting and got caught out in a freak winter storm. First his dog came home alone. Then they found his boat and the body of his hunting buddy. Several days later, they found Craig, stretched out on the ground the way you would if you were making a snow angel. He'd struggled out of the water and died of hypothermia, gazing up at the frozen sky.

The band vowed to play on—and they still do—but they never even considered replacing Craig, and truth be told, they'd lost that goofy innocence that was once the irresistible hallmark of their live shows. They were still bonded by brotherly love, but now their harmony has an ache in it, which gives it a whole different kind of beauty.

> They were still bonded by brotherly love, but now their harmony has an ache in it, which gives it a whole different kind of beauty.

I met Josh in 2016 when he played guitar at my niece's wedding. The first thing I noticed was what a very good

THERE BE THREE THINGS
which are too wonderful for me,
YEA, FOUR WHICH I KNOW NOT:

the way of an EAGLE IN THE AIR;

the way of a SERPENT UPON A ROCK;

the way of a SHIP IN THE MIDST OF THE SEA

and the way of a MAN WITH A MAID.

PROVERBS 30:18–19 KJV

musician he is. I was a weepy mess, of course, but I looked over at him, and even through my streaming eyes, I felt a frisson of talent turn-on—this thrill that goes through me whenever I see someone passionately practicing their art while also being hot. Josh goes to a rarified place when he plays, and I know that place—a combination of single-minded focus, muscle memory, and cane sugar high. When I'm in that place, I am my favorite version of myself. I recognized it in the music and in his face, later that day, when we talked about Pachelbel and Dolly Parton. He was shy and unshaven, easygoing in the most appealing way. And he was fourteen years younger than I.

"Cougar" is the kindest thing people say about a fifty-year-old woman who hooks up with a thirty-six-year-old man, and for some stupid reason, that mattered to me at the time. There are so few people who resonate with me in that particular musical sense, it would have been wrong to pretend we'd never met, but I decided we should be friends.

In 2018 my nephew got married. Once again, I was a weepy mess, all *sunrise, sunset, swiftly flow the years*, when I heard an unmistakable stroke of genius on the guitar.

Stop it, God. Stop. It.

I suddenly remembered that I don't give a crap what other people say about me, and Josh and I have been together ever since.

I consider myself lucky in love. I've had my heart broken by—and broken the hearts of—a few truly exceptional men. Personally and professionally, my life is rife with extraordinary circumstances, and the only men who get that live similarly complicated lives. The one thing Josh and I have that I never had with anyone else is time to be quiet.

In the winter of 2020, as the global pandemic descended and quarantine closed in around us, Broadway went dark, concert venues canceled everything, movie and TV filming came to an abrupt halt. Josh's studio and live gigs evaporated. We found ourselves in a silent place, and we were both terrified, but we were together.

We're both obsessed with what we do—workaholics, it's fair to say—so this was an incredibly difficult time for both of us. It was fraught. We had our moments. But even in the darkness, there was harmony. We sat in the bathroom in my New York apartment—because acoustics—and sang "Amazing Grace" while hospital orderlies carried body bags out to the refrigerator trucks across the street from my living room window.

Josh doesn't try to do alterations on me. I am who I am with him, and he's unabashedly delighted by it. He plays "Freebird" on request. He understands why I cry when Thunderpup isn't with me. We're soul-friends.

It's a good feeling.

Back in the day, when I was still in college, working toward my master's degree, I struggled through the endless blah blah blah of music theory, and I hated every minute until I clapped on to the science that explained everything I already understood on a gut level. I could sing harmony with anything on the radio. The harmony was just hanging there in the air, I thought. How could anyone *not* hear it? It frustrated me that some people looked at me like I was crazy and thrilled me when I got the knowing nod from others. We hear each other the way dogs hear a whistle at thirty thousand hertz.

> We hear each other the way dogs hear a whistle at thirty thousand hertz.

Harmony, according to music theory, is defined by a simultaneity perceived by your ear in the same way your eye perceives movement and pattern. Your brain is hardwired to receive information via the auditory nerve. Each musical note resonates at a certain frequency: C at 16.35 hertz, D at 18.35, E at 20.60, and so on.

When the frequencies are spaced at elegant intervals, in multiples of the fundamental note, it creates harmonics—or *consonance*—which triggers a pleasure response in the brain. When frequencies are spaced too close together, notes

We're
SOUL-FRIENDS.

end up stepping on each other's toes, stimulating the same auditory nerve fibers, creating *dissonance*, which sends a jarring message to your jangled brain, and your brain responds with stress hormones.

Like any great love affair, music features both vertical and horizontal components. The horizontal elements—melody and rhythm—are pretty straightforward. Think about an Irish tenor singing "Danny Boy" a cappella. The vertical element—harmony—brings depth, texture, and passion. Think about the heart-gripping intro to "Carry On Wayward Son" by Kansas or the sensuous soprano/alto liaison in Delibes "Duo des fleurs" from *Lakmé*.

> Like any great love affair, music features both vertical and horizontal components.

During the first two years of our relationship, Josh and I were elegantly spaced, each doing our own thing. He's the only significant other in my life who's never tried to architect me in some way.

I worried that quarantine would cram us into a dangerous proximity where we'd grind on each other's last auditory nerve fiber. And at times, we did. When the world began to open up again, I worried that the warm, simple home we'd made for ourselves would be torn apart by the demands of both our careers when all that noise and activity came roaring back like acid reflux.

But we were okay.

I was, and he was, and our *we* was okay.

Harmony isn't about matchy-matchy one-note sympatico. It's about the space between. It's about coming together in a way that pleases and perplexes at the same time, because without tension—without dissonance—the pleasure of consonance would be pale and shallow. Harmony is richer for the ache that comes before the resolution.

> Harmony is richer for the ache that comes before the resolution.

On a crisp late-autumn evening, on the rooftop above the Rainbow Room at Rockefeller Center, Josh got down on one knee and old-school proposed.

Over the Rainbow.

How cute is that?

On the nose, I know, but I loved it.

We don't know exactly what comes next, but we know it'll be built around music and sustained by love.

In the absence of noise, we found our vertical.

The horizontal ain't bad either.

From the insecurity that tells us love is weak,

from the cynicism that tells us love is rare,

from the naivete that tells us love is everything,

Good Lord, deliver us.

WHAT THE WORLD NEEDS NOW

FILL THIS HEART WITH EVERYTHING YOU LOVE.
I'LL GET IT STARTED WITH A FEW SUGGESTIONS.

spring
puppies
music
your awesome self

You are my sunshine,
my only sunshine.
You make me happy
when skies are gray.

BUT, HEY, I'M NOT AN IDIOT.

WHEN SKIES ARE GRAY,

I TAKE VITAMIN D.

Randomania

When I want a long day to be over,
I say, "Stab me with a dull butter knife."
It's like "Stick a fork in it, it's done."
But less pointed.

TS ABOUT
LOSS

John Sawyer was an exceptional performer who worked everywhere, made his Broadway debut in Frank Wildhorn's *The Civil War*, and was later one of the cofounders of my Broadway Bootcamp. We met in a church group when we were kids. We were teenagers when we did *Promises, Promises*—the show I revived on Broadway with Sean Hayes in 2010. We were in dance class together at OCU. We went to New York together, worked and played and bunked together, ate and drank and cried and played cards, kindred spirits who saw each other naked—emotionally, physically, financially, and musically.

I was John John's beard for a while and his sister friend for life, but honestly, neither of these descriptors truly captures the essence of our relationship. Over the years, whatever ad hoc families came and went as we worked in various shows and tours, John John was always part of my crew, and I was part of his. I have a brother through adoption and a brother and sister by blood, but in practical reality, John John was my soul sibling. He was a deeply good human being who made me a kinder, smarter, more stylish person.

Now, I checked this next part with Josh, who looked it up on his phone, so I know it was May 9, 2020. We were playing canasta, and I felt these words coming into my heart. I thought it was a song or poem coming to me, and I didn't want to lose the lines, but I didn't have anything to write it down, so I asked Josh to make a note on his phone.

I didn't wanna leave, but I couldn't stay.

Later, lying in bed, I listened to that untidy inner cosmos we call inspiration, allowing the words to flow, continuing the thread in my journal.

I wanna stay, but I have to go
It gets lonely, I bet you know
I'm above and I can see
Don't know why I couldn't stay down there
So much more I wanna share
You'll know when you feel warm and better
When you feel a chill
I'm gonna come visit you. I will.

The next day, a mutual friend called to tell me that John John had taken his own life.

Hearing these words on the telephone—I didn't feel it at first. Like that second it takes you to take your finger off a frying pan. A swift blade of shock severs your brain from your body.

Questions swarmed my brain, but I didn't ask *why*; I knew why. Something John and I had in common was an ongoing struggle with depression. I know how those long, dark hours grind you down and slap you stupid and whisper in your ear that God is waiting for you just on the other side of indecision. At that moment, in the middle of quarantine, with Broadway dark, so many friends sick and dying, families falling apart, proximity burn that had couples at each other's throats—how could anyone already prone to depression not feel as if they were trying to claw their way up from the bottom of a well?

Apply as Needed:

I know how to be BROUGHT LOW,

and I know how to ABOUND.

In any and every CIRCUMSTANCE,

I have learned the SECRET

of facing PLENTY *and* HUNGER,

ABUNDANCE *and* NEED.

I can do ALL THINGS THROUGH HIM

who STRENGTHENS ME.

PHILIPPIANS 4:12–13 ESV

The news of John's death threw me to the ground. I was stunned to wake up every morning, separated from him and from the life I loved—the life we shared—which could never be the same. Waves of sorrow and anger engulfed me in turn. I stood in the shower, weeping and cursing. *What the fuck! What the fuck! How could you do this, you dork? You could have held on to me—or given me the chance to hold on to you.* I kept thinking of that Jacques Brel song, "Ne me quitte pas"— *don't quit me, don't quit me, forget those hours that kill the heart of happiness . . .*

If I'd been there, I wondered, could I have sung him back into being in love with life? Was love not enough for people like us? Was love so powerless?

The brutal finality of this loss was the answer to these and many other questions. The magnitude of this loss laid my bones bare. The magnitude of my anger scared me. I woke up every morning with the bitterness of it in my mouth until one morning when I woke up to a text telling me to look outside. Jennifer Aspen, one of my amazing costars from *GCB*, was standing in the street below my balcony holding up a big sign.

If I'd been there, I wondered, could I have sung him back into being in love with life?

I LOVE YOU

I started crying, and she turned the sign around.

YOU ARE GOING TO BE OKAY

It's a process, singing someone back into love with life. It doesn't happen in a moment, but a moment like this is what that process is made of. This enormously kind gesture—the straightforward grace it takes to show up for someone—was more than the message, but that simple message is so profoundly important.

You are going to be okay.
YOU are going to be okay.
You ARE going to be okay.
You are going to be OKAY.

You, my dear second-person pronoun, *are going to be*, in a future that includes you, *okay*—which is not to say perfect. But fair to middlin' is better than the hole you're in now, right? It's a baby step toward being in love with your life again. It's a recognition that you are not okay now, and that—well, that sucks. Whatever it is you've lost, you won't get it back. It's gone. But something else will be revealed.

Like the title song says in *Promises, Promises*:

You
are
going
to be
okay.

Things that I promised myself fell apart.
But I found my heart.

Pain is our invitation to the privilege of empathy. And loss—that brutal SOB—is evidence of love. What a tragedy it would be if anyone were to make it through life unscathed by loss of such humbling magnitude. That would mean they never loved, which means they never truly lived at all.

> **Pain is our invitation to the privilege of empathy.**

If one good thing comes out of our recent global gut punch, I hope it's that the sorrowful state of our hug-deprived world shines a light on our interconnectedness, illuminating the power and importance of tiny, radical kindnesses.

**A SIMPLE PRAYER
FOR A LOST SOUL**

I bear ya.

At the end of the day, we can endure much more than we think we can.

FRIDA KAHLO

I will remember you.

INHALE THROUGH YOUR NOSE,
exhale through your mouth.

- Start with your arms crossed, giving yourself a hug.
- Hold both hands over your heart.
- Allow your thoughts to rest on the word *here*.
- Focus on the memory of someone you have loved and lost. Let images of them play across your mind like a slideshow, and invite that memory to remain in your heart.

TS ABOUT
ORTUNITY

A few weeks after John's death, my agent got a call from the Food Network, of all things. Honey, hush. I know I have kitchen appliances somewhere, but I'm not the type to make any substantial use of them. I consider it haute cuisine when a street vendor puts a scoop of chili in a bag of Fritos. Throw some shredded cheese on top of that, and it's Wolfgang Puck.

Nonetheless. The Food Network.

They, like many other studios, were desperately scraping together tiny production pods in which people were protected to the greatest extent possible—distancing, masks, sanitizer—every possible measure. They wanted me to host a life-size version of the game Candy Land.

Praise God from whom all blessings flow!

I climbed onto this opportunity like a life raft. Work has always been my therapy, my vehicle for survival, an irrefutable railroad track for that crazy train between groggy mornings and sleepless nights. When I work, I know who I am, so you better believe I was on that set in my six-inch heels and sneeze guard. Every day we got our noses probed like UFO abductees. Between takes, we wore cones of shame, like we were dogs who just got spayed and had to be prevented from licking our stitches. And we were thrilled to do it. *Thrrrrrrrilllllllllled*. I consumed mass quantities of sugar, consoled the losers, cried with the winners, and cherished every second of that sweet little *Candy Land* series.

When I got home, I had to quarantine hard, but Josh and I were in LA, where we had a bit more space. We converted my closet into a sound booth where I could do voiceovers and he could record music and do virtual session work. That's where I did the voice of Mary the mouse in the 2020 reboot of Roald Dahl's *The Witches*. Then I came out of the closet and entered the *Schmigadoon!* pod with a ridiculous lineup of stellar show folks, including my darling Alan Cumming, who roomed right next door to me.

My big moment came in episode 5: an eighteen-page patter song that our producer, Barry Sonnenfeld, wanted in one extended camera shot done in one take. The song—a send-up of "Ya Got Trouble" from *The Music Man*—is a four-minute, mostly spoken stream of rapid-fire lyrics leading up to a big choral finish with dance lifts, time steps, and a soaring signature high note, of course. The opportunity to execute something so elaborately choreographed, so technically precise, and so stinkin' hilarious was a dream come true. Or a nightmare. Could go either way. Go on YouTube and search "Schmigadoon!—Tribulation Singalong" if you want to give it a try. I dare you. (Please post and tag me on the video if you accept this challenge!)

I rehearsed the number night after night, dissecting the diction, deconstructing every phrase, parsing each line, individually, then in sections, then as a whole, over and over and over in front of the bathroom mirror until Alan was pounding on the wall, pleading for mercy.

Loud-mouthed trash with their tommyrot and flapdoodle
Claptrap and fiddle-faddle and jiggery-pokery.

I rehearsed it in my pj's and in my corset and wig. I rehearsed it in the shower. I rehearsed it in my sleep.

When it was finally time to shoot this complicated

If you think you can't,
you most certainly can't.

If you think you can . . .
well, I'd go with that.

WHAT DOES IT HURT?

number—one shot, one camera, one chance to get it right—
the set hummed with unified energy. I was at the center of it
all, but every single member of the cast and crew had to nail
every nanosecond of this thing with absolute clarity and on-
the-mark accuracy. Oh, please, watch the show, and notice
the priceless expression on every face in the chorus. Pay
attention to the specificity of every pompadour and the
stitching at the edge of every Edwardian sleeve. That camera
dolly rolls along, smoother than dextrose in a jellybean, in
perfect accord with that slipstream of brilliant lyrics.

> *Cows and sheep having amorous congress!*
> *Children with the mark of the beast on their foreheads!*

I was so intensely proud to be part of this extraordinary
company. What an opportunity.

For me, there is nothing as irresistible as a challenge in
which the opportunity to succeed is locked in amorous con-
gress with the opportunity to fail. Triumph and disaster hold
hands at the edge of a cliff. And . . . *jump.*

This is the twisted nature of opportunity.

Ask Emily Dickinson:

> "Success is counted sweetest
> By those who ne'er succeed."

Opportunity is a two-faced temptress. Yes, that new gig is an opportunity for advancement; it's also an opportunity to crash and burn. Yes, that gorgeous right swipe is an opportunity for happily ever after; it's also the opportunity for a mascara-dribbling walk of shame.

The courageous learn to flip that script.

Yes, that crash and burn is an opportunity to embarrass yourself; it's also an opportunity to learn, grow, and demonstrate how gracious you are under pressure. Yes, that walk of shame is the opportunity for disillusionment; it's also the opportunity to redefine your priorities and set the bar a little higher.

Yes, that pandemic is an opportunity for demoralizing loss and crushing loneliness; it's also the opportunity for you, your family circle, and the entire planet to refresh the air, look up from the status quo, and dig deep for creative ways to reinvent everything—communication, work, play, love, time, space—seriously! I mean everything, as in every stinkin' thing.

I'm not pretending it's easy. Opportunities for growth and development—personal and professional—often come in the context of a good old-fashioned ass-kicking. Opportunity has a consistently sick sense of humor. Sometimes you have to laugh.

There was no Broadway Bootcamp the summer of 2020, but after John's death, I was beyond determined to make it happen. All I could think about was the kid who was him when we met. John John told me more than many times what that bootcamp experience would have meant to him when he was a teenager trying to figure out where he was in terms of talent, possibility, sexuality, and real-time breaks. I also thought of Mama Lynn and the big dreams she had when she was a kid—dreams of doing all the things I eventually did. She had talent and creative potential that never found the space or resources to blossom.

"The technology is there to make it happen," I told Josh. "I gotta do it."

In order to optimize the student/teacher ratio, we'd always limited it to forty students. In 2021 more than a hundred kids from across the world came together for distance learning on a whole new level with high-caliber instructors (vaxxed and jacked) from Broadway and beyond. We had students from eight countries and thirty-three states. One incredibly talented young girl in the Philippines attended via an iPad that her community had pooled resources to buy for her. Three kids got signed by agents. I resisted the temptation to say, "Be careful what you wish for"—to both the kids and the agents—and promised God I would keep an eye on these precious children who'd found their way into my arms.

Oh, John John, I kept thinking. *If only you'd had the opportunity to see it.*

SHE STOOD
IN THE STORM
AND WHEN
THE WIND
DID NOT BLOW
HER WAY,
SHE ADJUSTED
HER SAILS.

ELIZABETH EDWARDS

So many opportunities to shine—standing at the edge of the cliff with opportunities to make a fool of oneself.

The final evening of Broadway Bootcamp is a celebration of everything we've all learned and contributed, so that's when I hand out the Kristi Awards. These are not participation awards; if you score a Kristi, it means you worked your butt off and created something special. Broadway Bootcamp, like Broadway itself, is a meritocracy; talent matters, effort is everything, and in the end, the only thing that counts is what happens on stage.

It was important to me that we include a meaningful tribute to BBC cofounder John Sawyer. I decided to sing "Days of Plenty" from *Little Women*, and thank the Lord, I had musical director John McDaniel at the piano, or I could not have gotten through it. I knew it would be hard, but I didn't understand how hard until I was standing there onstage in my sneakers, camo shorts, and BBC baseball shirt, thinking, *How did I think this was even possible?*

"Wow," I said, my throat full of emotion. "This happened. But certainly not by myself. There was the core. And in it—McD . . ." I turned to John McDaniel, hoping my eyes were telling him, *help me.* "With me was my friend . . . who you knew."

"Dear John," he said.

"John. Wasn't he a fantastic performer?"

"Amazing," said McD. "Amazing guy. So talented. Sweet. Handsome. Oh, gosh."

"Handsome!" I said wistfully. "He could eat me under the table."

By which I meant—like if you out-drink someone, you drink them under the table, right? Like I could eat a lot—of food!—and he could still eat me—no! I mean—you know what I meant! It just came out wrong, but—again, thank the Lord—I didn't pick up on this little fox paw, even though McD laughed a small, stunned laugh, glancing down at the keyboard.

"John Sawyer's not here with us on this planet anymore," I said, "but he continues to show himself to me, McD. And you know how he does it? Through the most vibrant rainbows I've ever seen."

Which is perfect, isn't it? Rainbows as a symbol of coming out and of hope renewed, as an artifact of *The Wizard of Oz* and the song no one and everyone could sing after Judy Garland sang it, but mostly as an opportunity to see something more than every single one of our favorite colors—the opportunity to see above and beyond and over the rainbow.

I felt John's laughter carrying me as I sang that impossible song:

There's got to be meaning . . . when a life has been so brief . . .
[He] will live in your bounty . . . as you carry on your life.

A SIMPLE PRAYER FOR OPPORTUNITY

Help me see it.

The passing lane to the left of status quo.

The place where the grace notes go.

A space for my song.

A need for my voice.

*The empty plate waiting for
my loving-kindness.*

*Let me dream an undreamed dream
and wake up wondering:*

How did I not think of that before?

*I'm just
trying to*
matter.

JUNE CARTER CASH

SHE'S A BRICK HOUSE

FILL EACH BRICK WITH SOMETHING THAT MAKES YOU FEEL
STRONGER. I'LL GET YOU STARTED WITH A FEW SUGGESTIONS.

WEARING THE
RIGHT SHOES

BIG HAIR

KNOWING I'M MY
MAMA'S DAUGHTER

PROTEIN

YOU BELIEVING
IN ME

TS ABOUT
ANXIETY

Fun fact: I hoard quarters. This deeply ingrained habit began when I was a college student. The laundry of a performing arts major is appalling in ways you might not readily imagine. You sweat. You dance, do improv, paint sets, and grub around on the floor, breathing from your belly, plus everybody spits when they sing. You work and work out, making a vain attempt at style the whole time, so, back then, the quarters were for the laundromat.

Later, as a busy New York theater bee, I needed the quarters for parking meters, newspapers, and pay phones, because you never know when you'll need to beef up your karma, read the dailies, or call your agent.

Nowadays, I just need them because quarters.

The pleasure of hoarding quarters is tinged with anxiety. I can't afford to get sick, so I've always been hypervigilant about bacteria, and nothing outside the snout of a feral pig is grimier than money. I sanitize my quarters with Purell the second I get them home.

But there's that moment when a quarter sits there on the palm of an outstretched hand. I want it. I want it so bad. Do I accept it with a smile and genuine thanks or cringe away with my hand in my pocket?

In philosophical terms—and in theater—this is the classic Apollonian/Dionysian conflict.

Apollo and Dionysus, both sons of Zeus, could not have been more at odds. Apollo was the smart kid, god of the sun, who reigned with rationality and logic. Dionysus was a frat boy, god of wine and dance, who reveled in chaos and emotionally charged, headbangers-ball hedonism. We precious humans need them both, and my quarter fetish tells you why.

The heart wants what it wants, and the brain is on board up to a point, but anxiety comes in with a long list of invisible—but very possible—preemptive threats, hidden dangers, horrific eventualities, and borrowed trouble. Cue the conflict.

My anxiety manifests in a character I call Patty Paranoid.

ME: Quarters! Yay!

PATTY: Two words: *Fecal. Bacteria.*

ME: But . . . quarters . . .

PATTY: Pathogens. Rhinovirus. Staphylococcus aureus.

ME: What's that?

PATTY: Flesh-eating bacteria.

ME: Liar. Full of lies. You just don't want me to be happy!

PATTY: Pseudonomas aeruginosa.

HEART: *Quarrrrrrterrrrrrs!*

BRAIN: Imploding. Imploding now.

PATTY: Bloody diarrhea. Kidney failure.

ME: Keep the change.

Now, this whole improv exercise takes place in a perfectly clean Starbucks. I can't see any reason to be standoffish, but Patty Paranoid is all about the unseen. What would she do with herself all day if I only worried about things that were, you know—*real*? And yes, flesh-eating bacteria is real, but there's no evidence that my latte is foaming with it.

Patty is all about the worst-case scenarios: the accident waiting to happen, the monster lurking under the bed. I haven't been able to convince her that the *real* worst-case

FAITH

is a reasonable stand-in for

COURAGE

scenario is a life unlived, a quarter unhoarded, a risk untaken, an experience unexplored. I've been trying to break up with Patty since my early teens, but she just keeps showing up at my doorstep.

I do have one thing going for me: faith.

Faith is a reasonable stand-in for courage.

I can't completely silence the raspy whisper of anxiety, but faith enables me to step off the curb.

Faith in God.

Faith in the folks who raised me.

Faith in the innate goodness of people.

Faith in myself.

That's the toughest one, isn't it? Finding or manufacturing—or faking—faith in yourself requires you to sum up all those other kinds of faith and surrender yourself—*Surrender, Dorothy!*—to the idea that you really do have resources sufficient to survive whatever it is you're afraid of.

It's a project—a decision followed by creative thought, strong intention, and strategic action.

Instead of spending another sleepless night salsa dancing with your self-doubt, take your ego out on a date. Woo your willpower. Romance your stubborn pride. Honor your anxiety as a first step toward letting it go.

Oh, God.

Here we go.

*Please note
use of plural
pronoun.*

Amen.

PARTIAL LIST OF TERRIFYING THINGS *THAT REALLY COULD HAPPEN, SO TRY NOT TO* THINK ABOUT IT

- SPLIT POSTERIOR PANTS SEAM

- INOPPORTUNE PROJECTILE VOMITING DUE TO BRAIN TUMOR

- BRAIN TUMOR

- CAT SCRATCH FEVER

- HEARING THE SONG "CAT SCRATCH FEVER" AND NOT BEING ABLE TO GET IT OUT OF YOUR HEAD

- IMPORTANT RELATIONSHIP DISRUPTED BY DEVASTATING REVERSAL

- IMPORTANT RELATIONSHIP CONTINUING UNTIL DEATH DO US PART

- DEATH

- TOM HANKS ANNOUNCING RETIREMENT

- PARENTS CONVERTING LIFE SAVINGS TO BITCOIN

- NO MORE QUARTERS

Randomania

You can wrestle with a pig,
but it's still a pig.
And it's happy.

MOST LIKELY LOCATION NEXT TIME I CRY

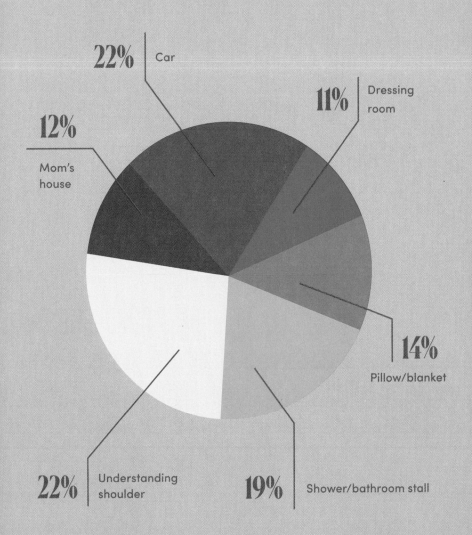

22% Car

11% Dressing room

12% Mom's house

14% Pillow/blanket

22% Understanding shoulder

19% Shower/bathroom stall

TS ABOUT
CLOSURE

I t was not for nothin' that they called 1967 the Summer of Love, and Billy Ethridge was positioned to make the most of it. He was handsome and unutterably cool, a savant musician who could shred the lead guitar, lay down bass, play keyboards, and even drum if he had to. He had the most ridiculous cadre of friends in the music world. When a high school classmate got drafted, Billy showed up at the going-away party with Don Henley in tow. He gigged with his buddy Stevie Ray Vaughan and played bass with The Chessmen, a band led briefly by Stevie Ray's brother, Jimmie.

The Chessmen were riding a wave, packing local hot spots

in Dallas and Houston, playing the Saturday morning teen shows on local TV, and opening for national touring acts including the Jimi Hendrix Experience and "all the invading English groups," as Billy put it. They flew in and out of Love Field in Dallas, so they flew Braniff.

The Summer of Love abruptly cooled off when Billy and one of his bandmates both fell in love with the same free-spirited stewardess. She turned up pregnant and didn't know which one of them was the father. The Chessmen broke up, succumbing to the drama, but a truly great bass player is never unemployed for long. Billy was recruited by his friend Billy Gibbons to join a new band Gibbons was putting together after his Moving Sidewalks bandmates got drafted. The band was called Texas at first, but then Gibbons changed the name to ZZ Top.

They had a good year, opening for Eric Burdon, Jimi Hendrix, Janis Joplin, and other big names, but they weren't able to score a record deal in the U.S. It's been reported that Billy left the band because he didn't want to sign a record deal with a London label, but in an interview with *Shindig!* in 2015, Gibbons said it was about the music. They were going for a guitar-driven Jeff Beck vibe; Billy wanted to play a Hammond B-3 double-keyboard organ, laying down the bass line with foot pedals. In the early days of ZZ Top—before the big-budget tour buses and road crew—gigging with guitars was a simple matter. Lugging that organ around was an expensive proposition.

They parted amicably, and Billy went on to play studio sessions and gigs and tour with Stevie Ray Vaughan. Through it all, he and his free-spirited Braniff girl stayed together.

She wasn't about to disappear the way pregnant girls were expected to disappear back then. She could have easily flown to Tijuana for a back-alley abortion, but that was a terrifying prospect and didn't work with her belief system. It wasn't the right choice for her. She didn't even know she was pregnant until she was three months along, and she worked for three months after that, keeping her terrible secret hidden inside her mod Pucci uniform.

Billy was willing to marry her and raise the baby as his own. He had this big idea that they could take the baby on the road with the band, but that didn't feel like the right choice either.

"I thought about raising you on my own with help from my parents," she told me. "My mother's best friend sat me down and made me see that this wouldn't be fair to my mama, who suffered terribly with vertigo and epilepsy."

Mama Lynn didn't want to burden her mother, knowing that her mother's life was already a struggle. At the same time, she knew she couldn't do this alone. Her mother's friend suggested adoption. This Christian lady said she just

THE WAY I SEE IT,
IF YOU WANT THE
RAINBOWS,
YOU GOTTA PUT UP
WITH THE RAIN.

DOLLY PARTON

knew a good family was out there somewhere waiting for this baby, and painful as it was, that did feel right to Mama Lynn. A lawyer facilitated the closed adoption, and nurses took me away the moment I was born. They didn't even let her hold me.

"That's how it was back then," she says.

Four days after she gave birth—as my parents held their breath at home in Broken Arrow—Mama Lynn's daddy took her to the courthouse in Tulsa to sign the documents that would make me somebody else's baby girl. She hoped her daughter would see someday that the ink was smudged with tears. She cried so hard, her daddy had to carry her out.

> She hoped her daughter would see someday that the ink was smudged with tears.

She fell into a hard depression, and it lasted a long time, but when she and Billy were both a little older, a little wiser, they ended up getting married. They had their individual struggles, but they loved each other and eventually had two children—Jennifer and Christopher—and stayed together for more than forty years. When Mama Lynn's daddy was on his deathbed, he told Jennifer about the baby girl who'd been given up for adoption. Jennifer registered her DNA in an adoption database.

And that's how The Locator located her.

When I first met Mama Lynn, she told me that she was certain Billy was not my biological father, but—long story short—paternity tests showed that he was. Suddenly I was the big sister instead of the little sister. I was nervous about telling Mom and Dad, but they met my extended family with open hearts. Mom made Mama Lynn a big book of photos—from baby pictures to Broadway—and spent hours answering her questions.

He wasn't all that old, but sometimes it's the mileage more than the years.

There wasn't much time for Billy and me to get to know each other. He wasn't all that old, but sometimes it's the mileage more than the years. Drinking and drug use—years of falling off the wagon and scrambling to get back on—had murdered his liver and kidneys and left him with a host of health issues.

"He's dying," Mama Lynn told me.

The day I met him, he had a hard time getting up off the couch, but he struggled upright and studied me with a gold-flecked version of my own hazel eyes.

"What's this note?" he asked, and then he sang a clear, sustained, "*hommmm*."

"That'd be a D," I said.

"What about this? *Hommmm*."

"G sharp."

"Yup." He nodded his approval. "She's mine."

Like me, Billy had perfect pitch. Apparently, I inherited his fine auditory nerve fibers, and I also got his hands, weirdly, but other than that, I am the Mini-Me of Mama Lynn. My little sister, Jennifer, got his height; she towers over me. Our little brother, Christopher, got his kindness and creative spirit, but also some of Billy's complicated nature. Before Billy died, he said to me, with genuine sorrow, "You got the best of me. They got the worst."

He was deeply troubled by this final reckoning with his old demons: the raw understanding of how much his family had suffered because of his substance abuse. Lugging a Hammond organ around is nothing compared to the burden of addiction and its legacy.

I hope he was able to make peace with it at the end.

He died in 2015 in the bosom of his family, surrounded by love and music. Every heart he'd ever broken was there, wide open, willing to let him in and let him go. His passing was a master class in forgiveness—a template for the applied art of unconditional love—exactly what the world needs now.

People ask me if all this brought me closure, which makes me wonder if I'm doing closure right. My questions have been answered, but it didn't really change anything. My parents are my parents: Junie and Jerry Chenoweth of Broken Arrow, Oklahoma.

I was born into the perfect storm, blessed with an innate musical ability and raised by people who had zero expectations or preconceptions about what a life in music might entail. One might think that it would be better for a musically inclined child to be raised by parents who were familiar with and connected to the music industry, but in fact, my parents' lack of knowledge in that area allowed me to evolve purely as myself with no influences other than role models I naturally gravitated to and embraced.

We tend to think closure is about making peace with people from our pasts, but in practice, it's about making peace with ourselves.

Will the circle be unbroken
By and by, Lord, by and by . . .

That old song fills me with such hope. It makes me think of Grandma Chenoweth and all the other family and friends whose stories are woven into my own.

"You don't understand, baby girl, who you are and where you came from," Mama Lynn tells me. "I'm just an old squaw lady woman. You don't get it."

But I think I kinda do. Or at least I have an inkling.

I got thoughts.

Even before I knew the facts of my DNA, I felt the Choctaw and Cherokee blood in my veins. I felt myself drawn to the art and music of that culture but didn't feel free to claim it out loud. One has to be sensitive. Politically correct. Where does this yellow-haired girl get off appropriating that heritage? But where does anybody else get off taking it away from me? Why shouldn't we be allowed to just be whomever we damn well think we are, or want to be, or can't help being—the way I was allowed to evolve musically—without the expectations or limitations placed on us by parents, peers, or the cultural cicada choir?

Don't be a drag, just be a queen, right?

I wonder if everything I don't know about my heritage somehow coincides with everything I've yet to discover about myself. Or if my Native American heritage is partially defined by the fact that so many of us have been disconnected from it.

This is where closure gets dicey; on a superficial level, it's the opposite of being open. At first glance, it's an ending instead of a beginning. But closure is more than the satisfaction of one's Nancy Drew curiosity. It's about accepting all that we don't know—and can't know—until we rejoin the universal spirit of God in the vast continuum of love that created us.

By and by, Lord. By and by.

That happened.

*Thank you, Lord, for
your mysterious ways.*

*Lead me forward now,
into the mystery of
myself.*

We are the opening verse
of the opening page
of the chapter of
ENDLESS POSSIBILITIES.

Rudyard Kipling

AFTERWORD

Josh plays a crazy-cool version of "Amazing Grace" unlike anything I've ever heard in the roughly 8,967,443 times we've all heard that song. The guitar is dropped to open D tuning, so the lower strings suggest the drone of bagpipes that originally defined that melody. The tempo begins with the traditional haunting adagio and then kicks up to a galloping allegro that invites me to ad-lib a countermelody, and as I do, my mind goes to grace—unplanned, unrecorded, unchained.

It's thrilling to experience this familiar song in a way that feels fresh and a little edgy. Every once in a while, in the practice room with my longtime pianist and music director, Mary Mitchell, something emerges and takes us by surprise. My voice continues to change in response to the changes in my body, my soul, and the environment around me. It's a metaphor for the changes we all ponder as we take in the gifts, regifts, and steady parade of white elephant *are you kidding me* gifts we continually receive from a loving God and mostly benevolent universe.

I get the same thrill when I revisit Rumi, Emily Dickinson,

Shakespeare, or the Bible and stumble across something that strikes a completely unexpected chord. We should always be ready to question our faith.

Faith is another word for fearless. It welcomes the harmony of doubt and the countermelody of new ideas.

Consider. Reconsider. Repeat.

I hope this little book sparked your doubts and ideas while creating a safe place for your faith. And I hope you'll keep it in a shoebox or memorabilia bin—wherever you store your personal time-capsule treasures—so you can come back to it years from now and hear the voice of your younger self in the margins.

That person you hope to be is already within you.

When you do circle back to check in with the person you are now, remember to be kind. Remember that we see time as a horizontal line, but in fact, eternity is vertical, an ever-upward path toward grace. The never-ending now—wherever you are in this moment—is the palm of God's hand.

May joy and peace be with you.

ACKNOWLEDGMENTS

God knows I love my extended family, who are more of an amoeba than an unbroken circle: Mom, Dad, Mama Lynn, siblings, cousins, and all the beautiful people—too numerous to mention—who populate our holiday gatherings, especially those who bring pie. You know who you are. I'm also blessed with a wildly creative posse of excellent friends. I'm afraid to name names because I'll start crying and miss someone. Please know that I see you, and I'm grateful.

It takes a dynamic team to create a good book, and I have a great one: huge thanks to Danielle Peterson, Bonnie Honeycutt, and the talented team at HarperCollins who embraced this idea and helped me launch this little paper sailboat into the world. I'm blessed to be in the capable hands of my agent, Richard Abate, and his crew at 3 Arts Entertainment. My assistant, Jordan Gross, is like a barrel rider in the ongoing rodeo of my career. My collaborator Joni Rodgers consistently spins straw into gold with support from Patty Lewis Lott and Cindi Davis-Andress. Thank you, thank you, thank you all for making me sing on paper.

Josh Bryant, I'm deeply grateful for your love and support through quarantine and beyond.

Last but not least, to my Glitter Girls, all the brilliant kids at KCBBC, and fabulous fans all over the world: your love and energy are my jet fuel. I appreciate you every day. Keep living wickedly. See you on Broadway!

ABOUT THE AUTHOR

Emmy– and Tony Award–winning actress and singer Kristin Chenoweth's career spans film, television, voiceover, and stage. She received an Emmy Award for Best Supporting Actress in a Comedy Series for her role in *Pushing Daisies*, won a Tony Award for *You're a Good Man, Charlie Brown*, and received a Tony Award nomination for her original role of Glinda the Good Witch in the Broadway smash-hit *Wicked*. Chenoweth has released multiple albums, including *The Art of Elegance* and *For the Girls*, and has performed to sold-out audiences across the world. Kristin stars in the Apple TV+ musical comedy series *Schmigadoon!* She also starred in the Netflix comedy feature *Holidate*, voiced the character Daisy in the HBO Max film *The Witches*, and hosted the Food Network series *Candy Land*. Kristin remains a passionate supporter of charities, including the Broken Arrow Performing Arts Center Foundation in her home state of Oklahoma, where she launched an annual Broadway Bootcamp providing young Broadway hopefuls with the opportunity to learn from mentors in the field.